*Emerson as Mythmaker*

# *Emerson as Mythmaker*

By

J. RUSSELL REAVER

*RWE*

UNIVERSITY OF FLORIDA PRESS
*Gainesville*
1954

*To*

*My Mother and Father*

*A University of Florida Press Book*

Copyright, 1954, by the University of Florida
*All rights reserved*

Library of Congress Catalogue Card No.: 54-8431

Manufactured by Rose Printing Company, Inc.
Tallahassee, Florida

# Acknowledgments

PERMISSION TO QUOTE copyrighted material is gratefully acknowledged to publishers as follows: American Book Company: *A History of American Letters*, by Walter F. Taylor. Appleton-Century-Crofts, Inc.: *Creative Mind*, by Charles E. Spearman. Chatto & Windus, Ltd.: *Seven Types of Ambiguity: A Study of Its Effects in English Verse*, by William Empson. Dodd, Mead & Company: *Psychology of the Unconscious: A Study of the Transformations and Symbolisms of the Libido, A Contribution to the History of the Evolution of Thought*, by Carl G. Jung. Duke University Press: Review by Norman Foerster, in *American Literature*, of Ralph L. Rusk's *The Life of Ralph Waldo Emerson*. Farrar, Straus & Young, Inc.: *The Psychoanalyst and the Artist*, by Daniel E. Schneider. University of Florida Press: *Cosmic Optimism: A Study of the Interpretation of Evolution by American Poets from Emerson to Robinson*, by Frederick W. Conner. Greenberg: Publisher: *Freud: His Dream and Sex Theories* (originally titled *The House That Freud Built*), by Joseph Jastrow. Harcourt, Brace & Company: *Modern Man in Search of a Soul*, by Carl G. Jung. Harper & Brothers: *Creative Vision in Artist and Audience*, by Richard Guggenheimer; *Tess of the D'Urbervilles*, by Thomas Hardy. Harvard University Press: *Philosophy in a New Key: A Study in the Symbolism of Reason, Rite, and Art*, by Susanne K. Langer; *The Transcendentalists: An Anthology*, edited by Perry Miller. The Hogarth Press, Ltd.: *Collected Papers*, by Sigmund Freud. Houghton Mifflin Company: *The Complete Poetical Works of William Wordsworth*, edited by Andrew J. George; *The Com-*

*plete Works of Ralph Waldo Emerson,* Centenary Edition, edited by Edward W. Emerson; *The Dance of Life,* by Havelock Ellis; *The Journals of Ralph Waldo Emerson,* edited by Edward W. Emerson and Waldo E. Forbes; *Movement and Mental Imagery,* by Margaret F. Washburn. The State University of Iowa: "The Manuscript Relationships of Emerson's 'Days,'" by Carl F. Strauch, in *Philological Quarterly.* The Lindsey Press: *The Religious Philosophy of Plotinus and Some Modern Philosophies of Religion,* by William R. Inge. Longmans, Green & Company, Inc.: *Memories and Studies,* by William James; *Theory and Art of Mysticism,* by Radhakamal Mukerjee; *The Works of John Ruskin,* edited by E. T. Cook and Alexander Wedderburn. The Macmillan Company: *Essays,* by William Butler Yeats; *Symbolism, Its Meaning and Effect,* by Alfred N. Whitehead. New Directions: *Seven Types of Ambiguity: A Study of Its Effects in English Verse,* by William Empson. Oxford University Press: *The Complete Poetical Works of Percy Bysshe Shelley,* edited by Thomas Hutchinson; *The Poetic Image,* by Cecil Day-Lewis; *The Poetical Works of Wordsworth,* edited by Thomas Hutchinson. Sampson Low, Marston & Company, Ltd.: *Emerson in Concord,* by Edward Waldo Emerson. Simon & Schuster, Inc.: *Modern Art: The Men, The Movements, The Meaning,* by Thomas Craven.

I am also indebted to Dr. Frederick C. Prescott, for excerpts taken from *The Poetic Mind* and *Poetry and Myth;* to Dr. Elisabeth Schneider, for an excerpt taken from *Aesthetic Motive;* and to Dr. Lionel Trilling, for an excerpt taken from "Freud and Literature," in *Criticism: The Foundations of Modern Literary Judgment,* edited by Mark Schorer, Josephine Miles, and Gordon McKenzie, later published in revised form in his collection, *The Liberal Imagination.*

No book, I imagine, has ever been the exclusive product of its author. For helpful criticism I am grateful to my colleagues Dr. Mary A. Magginis, Dr. William P. Randel, and Dr. J. Paul Stoakes of the English Department and Dr. Ralph M. Dreger of the Psychology Department at The Florida State University. Cordial recognition is likewise due to my former professors Dr. Leonard B. Beach and Dr. Harlan H. Hatcher because of their challenging guidance of my early Emerson study for the doctoral degree at The Ohio State University. But especially to my wife I wish to express my appreciation of her keeping a home in which this book could be written.

J. R. R.

*Tallahassee, Florida*
*February 3, 1954*

# Contents

"*There is never a beginning, there is never an end, to the inexplicable continuity of this web of God, but always circular power returning into itself.*"

— RALPH WALDO EMERSON

"*I have often had the fancy that there is some one Myth for every man, which, if we but knew it, could make us understand all he did and thought.*"

— WILLIAM BUTLER YEATS

# CHAPTER I

## *The Personal Myth*

INSPIRATION ARISES from the concentration of the whole
self on a point of interest. Since this book, intended for
the modern reader familiar with the poetry of Ralph Waldo
Emerson, is concerned with the ways of creative activity
in the intuitive mind of Emerson, as compared with the
typically rationalistic contemporary mind, it examines at
the outset those recent theories of the nature of man and
his creative imagination which have shaped the attitudes of
modern readers toward the artist and the sources of his
inspiration. In certain ways Emerson anticipated psychological interpretations of the whole self of man, yet he
differs significantly from some of the beliefs held by such
psychologists as Sigmund Freud or Carl G. Jung. This study
begins, then, with current concepts of man and his creative
life as they bear particularly on Emerson's evaluation of the
human being in his role as creator. Contrary to much modern thought, Emerson believed man's imagination springs
from ultimately reliable intuitive sources existing constantly
in human nature. Only intuition can plumb these creative
depths beyond the reach of conscious searching. At the
same time Emerson was convinced that the consciousness
of man, aware of the value of unconscious intuitional life,

1

could work in critical harmony with it to create a perfect projection of the whole man.

The imagination reveals itself in using materials to create a world of its own. Emerson constructs his imaginative visions, his personal myths, through using varied materials that his intuitive self directs through characteristic links and patterns. To examine the magazine of materials projected from an artist's mind is to see the results of the total creative energies at work. This volume thus investigates the use of images in Emerson's poetry, which is fundamentally lyrical but wider than the biographical self as Emerson projects his mythical vision of intuitional life through identifying man and his universe in a continuous creative effort. Unlike many poets of the mid-twentieth century, Emerson feels at home in his world.

Believing that the human self is innately admirable and that man lives in a favorable universe, Emerson was free to allow his intuitional imagination to give significant form to the deepest impulses of life expressed through charged images projected through sounds and rhythms organic to the creative energies of all life. The finished fabric of an Emerson poem thus becomes a kind of multiple metaphor of human life, a rhythmical myth spun, as Emerson might say, in the vast web of God. If modern man is willing to identify himself imaginatively with Emerson's confident vision of intuitive life in which idea and art become one, he may yet discover life has a meaning and direction that the exclusively rationalistic self can not know.

At all events, the modern reader who recognizes Emerson's historical importance and who seeks to re-create his work in the twentieth-century world may find, I believe, much significance in his imaginative vision. Beginning with the present intellectual atmosphere, largely conditioned by what is called scientific thought, this approach has peculiar virtue in its attempt to discover in what ways current ideas may be useful in arriving at a fuller appreciation of Emerson's point of view toward the creative life.

In this sort of endeavor the critic may aid the reader to achieve added insight into the values of a writer's work. As William Empson says in *Seven Types of Ambiguity*, "... conscious theory may make an addition to sensibility."[1] The critic appears less as a judge or historian than as a guide who hopes to share his more significant experiences and opinions with his reader. The critic thus leads to a more complete awareness of the continuing life in a work of art. A basic difference probably between the ordinary reader and the artist exists in just this acute awareness of life's inner movements and qualities.[2] "Criticism is an art," Emerson says, "when it does not stop at the words of the poet, but looks at the order of his thoughts and the essential quality of his mind."[3] The re-creative critic advances the reader toward participating more fully in the artist's projection.

In projecting something of himself in his writing, an author creates his own world of the imagination; he sees life from his angle of vision. The challenging problem of understanding the ways of the human imagination will be investigated later. At the moment we may note the suggestive comment of Freud, who remarked in his essay on "The Poet and Day-Dreaming" that the writer is not unlike the child at play: "... he creates a world of phantasy which he takes very seriously; that is, he invests it with a great deal of affect, while separating it sharply from reality."[4] Indeed the poet may regard his imaginative projections as more worthy of belief or filled with more value than everyday reality, as Wordsworth implies in his "Elegiac Stanzas Suggested by a Picture of Peele Castle" when he wishes he had the power

> *To express what then I saw; and add the gleam,*
> *The light that never was, on sea or land,*
> *The consecration, and the Poet's dream.*[5]

As we approach the problem of the creative imagination, an understanding of an author's use of imagery is essential. The study of imagery is probably one of the most rewarding ways of appreciating a writer's intentions, for the amount of thought or emotion with which the writer can invest an image is a valuable index to his poetic purposes. Particularly in Emerson's poems the image is the essence of poetry, and his imagery is perhaps one of his greatest contributions to American literature.

While placing emphasis on the use of images in creative literature, we should not overlook the fact that there are very probably some imageless processes of thought; Margaret F. Washburn maintains, in fact, that the faster the thought process, the less likely it is to depend on images and that "... a process may be imageless to introspection, and yet have the same kind of physiological basis as ordinary sensations."[6] It may also be true, as Charles E. Spearman believes, that imageful persons show no superiority over the imageless. Generally speaking, "... the persons who possess images of great vividness seem after all not to make much genuine usage of them."[7] In his *Principles of Literary Criticism*, I. A. Richards further asserts that the production of images is not necessarily involved in imaginative processes.[8] At all events an image as it appears in creative literature tends to be separate from what psychologists call an "eidetic image," the literally "seen" object of subjective visual experience, which may nevertheless differ in various details from the object represented.

As we all know, poems do vary in the degree of attention given to images as a means of communication, but, by and large, poets seem characteristically to communicate often in terms of images. When this is so, we may approach the essence of the poet's emotions and ideas by perceiving life through the symbolic representation of it in his images. As Cecil Day-Lewis says, ". . . metaphor remains, the life-principle of poetry, the poet's chief test and glory."[9]

The artist may often use quite unexpected materials and invest them with new significance. As we shall see, to Emerson every fact in nature may be taken as the basis for any generalization a writer may care to make; nothing is too small or mean to be used by the creative artist. The reason for this unexpected use of commonplace material is still largely mysterious. When describing the genius of Van Gogh, Thomas Craven remarks in *Modern Art: The Men, The Movements, The Meaning:* "How it is that certain minds seize upon materials which to most of us are commonplaces, remake and dramatize them, and invest them with the magic of a rich and unique personality, is as mysterious as life itself."[10]

Everyone sees nature or life as through a glass darkly because what he experiences is constantly colored by his needs and desires. As Henri Bergson maintains, what seems a clear view of external reality may be only that which one has selected from it to guide his conduct, and what seems a revelation from the heart may be only what one has known of his inner self as it played on the surface momentarily in his actions.[11] Not only the artist but everyone sees the world from his individual angle of vision. In this sense, each man creates his own world.

The artist may assist us, however, to increase our participation in life by helping us to become more aware of possible significances, by allowing us to experience life through the artist's greater sensitivity. What the artist succeeds in expressing, on the other hand, should not be thought of as representing all of his experience but only that part of life he is moved to express. Thomas Hardy understood this characteristic of an artist's nature when he said: "Differing natures find their tongue in the presence of differing spectacles. Some natures become vocal at tragedy, some are made vocal by comedy, and it seems to me that to whichever of these aspects of life a writer's instinct for expression the more readily responds, to that he should allow it to respond. That before a contrasting side of things he remains undemonstrative need not be assumed to mean that he remains unperceiving."[12] An artist's work is not equivalent to his biography; it is only what he has chosen to reveal imaginatively, or, as psychologists might say, only what the organism has selected consciously and unconsciously.

Only in the widest sense, then, may we consider the images a writer uses as deriving from his personal experience. The materials he uses may be the combined result of both immediate and vicarious experiences. It is not logical to say that every image a poet uses was the direct result of a personal experience. On the other hand, whatever appears in a poet's images must logically come from his total store of information and experience, from the reservoir of his conscious or unconscious being. This fund may be the product of his firsthand experience, the events of his personal life; or it may contain much secondhand experience from a vicarious, imaginative identification of himself with others, from his participating in the imaginative projections of life in literature, or, much less probably, as Jung came to believe, from a sort of common collective mind.

Generally speaking it matters less what the origin of particular images may be than what the terms are under which the poet expects us to take part in his projected experience as communicated through his images. It may be instructive to try to discover how the writer is using his materials, whatever they are.

If we are interested in undertaking such a study, we shall find that, on the whole, lyric poetry is rather more susceptible to such analysis than dramatic poetry. For in dramatic writing we have the double complexity of trying to consider both what directions the imagery takes because of the author's "subjective" choices and what directions may be determined principally by the author's awareness of the "objective" reality appropriate to the dramatic character, whose personality may be radically different from the dramatist's.[13]

Granted the precautions that the critical reader must take, the artist's final choices of imagery, especially in lyrical poetry, do reveal his interests and attentions; they represent those materials that have become significant for him because of their emotional or intellectual associations, conscious or unconscious. The creative act, according to Théodule Ribot, must first arise from a need, which arouses associations of images and objectifies them in an appropriate form.[14] These associations appear to be quite unpredictable. There may be many unconscious associations in the writer's imagination, creating its own illusions of life.

Although it is impossible to reduce all the ways of the

imagination to laws, the mind does follow, it would seem, two general processes of drawing analogies. These methods are personification and transformation.[15] Personification is essentially a projection from the inner to the outer world. All becomes as we are (or suppose ourselves to be). The world becomes significant because it seems analogous to human life. In personification, any aspect of the world, animate or inanimate, assumes some human characteristic. Turning to transformations, we discover they are of two kinds: first, the metamorphosis of one object (or thing) into another object (or thing); a cloud becomes a sailboat, the sky becomes the ocean, such transformations occurring because of general similarities among objects; and second, the metamorphosis of some object to resemble or symbolize an emotional or intellectual concept because some aspect of the object is believed to represent the abstract characteristic. The perception of the object, in other words, generates a psychological stirring, as it were, so that the object (or some part of it) becomes associated with the emotion or idea and comes to be a concrete equivalent for the psychological abstraction; a fox represents cunning, a dove represents peace, and the like. As we shall see, there is abundant evidence in Emerson's poetry of personification, as he reads aspects of himself into nature, and of transformation, as he is fascinated by the resemblances among parts of nature that to him suggest the unity of life. In his *Journals* Emerson noted, "That Nature works after the same method as the human Imagination. That Nature makes flowers, as the mind makes images. . . . That organic matter, and mind, got from the same law, so correspond."[16]

In its inventive role, the creative imagination appears to work in two principal ways, through condensation and displacement.[17] In condensation the imagination forms composite groupings consisting of elements from many original impressions. The organic, unified result, of course, will be a complex fusion of many associations, each original element carrying with it something of its original significance, but taking on new meanings from its organic relationships to the whole. This ability to condense many elements from varied sources gives intensity to the imaginative creation. The imagination works differently in displacement. Because of the many associations that may exist in the mind, an impression that at first may have seemed dominant may be displaced by another with which it has become associated. The displacement would seem to occur because of the greater psychic significance attached to the displacing element, perhaps quite unconscious to the writer. In poetic production, then, the poet may seem alternately to conceal and reveal. The more obvious association that we might expect may have been displaced by some other of personal significance to the author. In Emerson's thinking, for example, nature itself appears to operate alternately by concealment and revelation as nature "communicates" to man. Actually, of course, we are dealing with the problems of subjective and objective reality. Nature may appear to symbolize itself, yet nature also assumes the significance that the subjective imagination gives to it.[18]

Through these methods of the imagination the reader is stirred to participate imaginatively in the poem; his psychological responses are aroused. The esthetic creator, as Washburn points out, produces images whose movements remain concealed within the person who contemplates his work. These movements on which mental imagery rests are tentative and limited within the self.[19]

The creation of images is, of course, not limited to the poet. Such creation, in fact, is a central human activity. Although some symbols may be disturbing to personality development, it appears generally valid, as Radhakamal Mukerjee says, that the creation of images and symbols is an activity by which man creates an ideal world beyond the natural world: "He constantly creates images and symbols from which he derives as much satisfaction as he obtains from physical objects. Symbolization represents the process of substituting relatively simple and concrete images for those which are complex and abstract. Every symbol which grows and lives in the individual or the race satisfies and stabilizes a complex group of ideas, impulses, and interests. It, therefore, subserves a more effective and satisfactory adaptation to environment and is hence in keeping with a harmonious development of the personality."[20]

The linked associations of images are the results, then, of various interests. As a matter of fact, only the interesting parts of any event survive, centrally or peripherally; that is, only those parts that have affected us pleasantly or painfully.[21] This principle underlies the revival of images. Also the imagination may draw upon recent matters but usually chooses elements from the past; for imaginative uses it still seems, as Wordsworth said, emotion needs to be "recollected in tranquillity." Recent emotions generally lead to practical action, not to imaginative projection.[22] Using materials that have become significantly linked with psychological responses, the imagination draws on many elements from past and present. "Have you not found memory an apotheosis or deification?" asks Emerson. "The poor short lone fact dies at the birth. Memory catches it up into her heaven, and bathes it in immortal waters. Then a thousand times over it lives and acts again, each time transfigured, ennobled."[23]

These associations, largely noticed in voluntary thought, are usually unnoticed in involuntary or intuitive thought. The unconscious self does the work. To the intuitive poet, therefore, the results of the imagination impress him as being "given"; they arise from something more deeply buried than his conscious thought. Not having to notice the bonds of imaginative associations, the intuitive poet may gain greater freedom and scope than would be likely if he were relying mainly on voluntary, conscious thought.[24] The poem may thus appear to be what is often called "inspired" because its original materials arose spontaneously. As we shall see, the basic intuitions according to Emerson arise from unconscious sources; in this belief Emerson tends to agree with psychologists who maintain an identity between "intuitive" and "unconscious."

The many ways in which the writer may project himself into the outer world and may also produce analogies, through which he metamorphoses life, reveal the possibilities of unity and variety of imaginative creation, while intensity and complexity occur through the mind's methods of condensation and displacement. It is probably impossible ever to know entirely why such combinations are made or exactly how they are fused. To understand more fully we would need to know all the details of an author's most private life. Even then we would still be confronted with the operations of the unconscious self, probably more unpredictable than those of the conscious self.

In broadest terms the poetic creation appears to rise from concentrated emotional stirrings of the depths of a poet's life. This excitement leads to free, spontaneous ideas flowing one into another not unlike the unhampered associations of

a dream. These visionary ideas are likely to present themselves in the forms of concrete images with which they
have become associated or fused in the unconscious self, of
which more will be said later. From these images that have
arisen, the free play of the imagination creates a subjective
world, in some ways similar to the objective or external
world from which it has been derived, but different from
it because it has now been molded by the multiple psychological attitudes of the personal self that have given new
and individual emphases to the original impressions. The
resultant imaginative fusion will appear satisfying to the
poet since its organic unity has resulted from his most
deeply felt needs and desires; it is most fully his true self
that has been realized through its projection. Regardless of
how varied the images may seem, the unifying power is the
psychological need to express a satisfying whole.[25] "Inspiration" may therefore be regarded as originating in an unusual
concentration of the total self on a point of interest. This
intensification may arouse the deeper strata, as it were, of
the mind and produce an extraordinarily rich and significant
expression.[26] Emerson's method of writing illustrates this
point. He concentrated on a subject, planting it in his mind
so to speak, and then waited for ideas and concrete illustrations to arrive, as a bee comes to a rose. Like Wordsworth,
according to the experience he described in "I Wandered
Lonely as a Cloud," Emerson found images occurring:
"They flash upon that inward eye/Which is the bliss of
solitude."[27]

The poet's imagined world, then, in the sense used here,
issues from his power as a personal mythmaker, for he has
projected an imaginative interpretation that has validity only
because it is a unified expression of the self from which it

came. The associations or analogies that may be central in this projection of the personal myth may have little, if any, direct relation to objective reality. *Myth*, in relation to its origin within the individual creator, may thus be defined as characteristic of a subjective quality resulting from an imaginative interpretation of the "real world."

Any poem may be described as a result of the total combined thought and feeling of the poet; more specifically we mean that the poet's conscious intellect is always likely to be variegated by the tones of the unconscious emotional aspects of his being. In this way the poet's self is integrated. Although it is often difficult to perceive a complete division between idea and emotion, between the unconscious, "emotional" self and the conscious, "rational" self,[28] it is clear, nevertheless, to any sensitive reader of poetry that either emotion or intellect is dominant. Or, to put it differently, the poetic product will appear to be largely either outpourings of the deeply felt needs and impulses of the unconscious self or controlled and balanced expressions modified by the conscious mind seeking approval. Such a distinction is basic between a "romantic" writer, who projects himself quite freely, say like Whitman, and a "classical" one, who uses more restraint. As we will see, in Emerson intuition and intellect form an inseparable team.

It is the desire to appeal to public approval that gives rise to the use of the more traditional materials and forms. These forms will vary according to the independence of the poet and the notions of what is proper in the historical age. For example, Rosemond Tuve's study of Renaissance writers is concerned with their historical practices to achieve social response and approval for Elizabethan or metaphysical imagery.[29] The conscious control of social standards regulated the final use of these kinds of Renaissance imagery.

At all events, the creative thinker must express himself by means of the materials he knows best. Like other creative workers, a poet will use as the ingredients of his art those aspects of nature and man that life has stored in his mental equipment. As we recall, it does not especially matter in this study what is the origin of these materials. The elements of the poet's art, at any rate, are subject to his controlling ideas and emotions; it is in discovering his methods of using the basic stuff of his poetry that we find the poet's essential personality revealed. In this way we succeed in appreciating his personal myths, his imaginative visions. Often thinking in terms of imagery, the poet will give us insight not only incidentally into something of the range of his experience but more importantly into what we call the character of his mind. The tone and temper of the poet's being will determine what impressions are retained and later variously used to suggest in poetic images his interpretation of life. The poet of the first order who, in Ruskin's words, can "feel strongly, think strongly, and see truly"[30] successfully presents in metaphor a psychic reconstruction of the physical world that graphically conveys to us his inmost self. To create, of course, is not simply to select and rearrange our materials; to create is to reconstruct the existing state of things, bringing to life something that has never before existed. "Therefore we love the poet, the inventor, who in any form, whether in an ode or in an action or in looks and behaviour, has yielded us a new thought. He unlocks our chains and admits us to a new scene."[31]

## CHAPTER II

## *The Springs of Imagination*

IN *Observations on the Growth of the Mind* (1826), a work that Emerson valued highly and that remained popular with his followers for many years, Sampson Reed presented much of the literary theory that Emerson was to follow, particularly in its emphasis on the poet's need to rely on his deepest intuitions and allow nature, as it were, to speak through him. In surrendering himself, the poet receives direct expressions from the central creative energies of life, already partially revealed in the organic relationships of external nature itself. As Reed says, nature was "precisely and perfectly adapted to invigorate and strengthen the intellectual and moral man."[1] Poetry is one of the spontaneous expressions of the mind and discloses kinds of "truth"; in its projection through images, poetry operates on a basic creative principle, according to Reed. As Emerson was to say later in his section on "Language" in *Nature* (1836): "Have mountains, and waves, and skies, no significance but what we consciously give them when we employ them as emblems of our thoughts? The world is emblematic. Parts of speech are metaphors, because the whole of nature is a metaphor of the human mind."[2] In religious vein Reed defines the images of the outer world,

15

which become part of the poet's equipment, as the concrete language in which the creator speaks:

By poetry is meant all those illustrations of truth by natural imagery, which spring from the fact, that this World is the mirror of Him who made it. Strictly speaking, nothing has less to do with fiction than poetry. The day will come, and it may not be far distant, when this art will have another test of merit than mere versification, or the invention of strange stories; when the laws by which poetry is tested will be fixed and immutable as the laws of science; when a change will be introduced into taste corresponding to that which Bacon introduced into philosophy, by which both will be confined within the limits of things as they actually exist. It would seem that genius would be cramped; that the powers of invention would be destroyed; by confining the human mind, as it were, at home, within the bounds which nature has assigned. But what wider scope need it have? It reaches the throne of God; it rests on his footstool. All things spiritual and natural are before it. There is as much that is true as false; and truth presented in natural imagery, is only dressed in the garments which God has given it.[3]

Is this sort of rejoicing in confining the mind to the operations of nature only idealistic optimism, or can we still give some genuine credence to it?

As every student of Emerson knows, the influence of Plato as well as German idealism through Coleridge and elements of Oriental spirituality contributed to Emerson's thinking. In general the idealistic tradition has seen an intimate connection between matter and spirit; it places, perhaps most strongly in Oriental idealism, the precedence on spirit, matter being regarded as the illusion of finality. Indeed William R. Inge points out that in the philosophy of

Plotinus, whom Emerson much admired, the "soul" of man depends on a higher source: "The Soul creates in knowing, and knows by creating; it stamps itself on Matter, and is reflected in Matter. But the Soul itself, and its world, are wholly dependent on that great spiritual world of eternal existence and eternal activity, which are the object of the Soul's worship, the source from which it flowed, and the goal to which it strives to return."[4] Inge also stresses the belief that the discoveries of scientific laws are after all only hints of the essential unity between mind and matter: "The laws which the scientist thinks that he finds in Nature are the work of his own mind, which notwithstanding finds itself *in* those objects which are its own image, and more remotely the image of its own Author."[5]

In the light of these general interpretations of man and his creative efforts, how can more recent thinking help us toward an understanding of Emerson's work?

When the modern reader approaches any discussion of the workings of the imagination, he is bound to consider something of the various notions of Freud and Jung, who have influenced recent thinking in many ways. As a matter of fact, in her study of T. S. Eliot, Elizabeth Drew sees a number of parallels between the psychological concepts of Jung and the poetic processes of Eliot.[6] Let us look briefly at some of the present-day psychological attitudes toward man and his creative life to observe some of the elements present in our contemporary mental atmosphere, as we may call it, that may color our approach to the problem of reading any earlier writer.

Every informed reader of literature will recall at least the more popular aspects of the Freudian attitude, involving the picture Freud paints of the human psyche with the ego

and the super-ego arising out of the id and his emphasis
on the repressed desires of the individual emotional life. In
Freudian terminology, we remember, the unconscious part
of the mind is the completely submerged portion, contain-
ing urges and drives forgotten or ignored by the conscious
part of the mind, while the preconscious, which some psychologists call the subconscious, contains what is only tem-
porarily out of consciousness. The id contains the primitive
emotional drives of the person and is located in the unconscious. Although it has some unconscious functions as well,
the ego may generally be thought of as the heart of the
conscious life, and the super-ego is equivalent to what we
usually call the "conscience" of man. Repression involves
some forgetting of a desire of the id; it is buried in the
unconscious.

According to Freud, the id is "non-moral," the ego
strives to be "moral," or at least to abide by the demands
of internal and external "reality," and the super-ego is not
only "moral" but may become ruthlessly "hyper-moral."[7]
The pleasure-principle, reigning in the id, is substituted by
the reality-principle of the ego in its attempt to bring the
tendencies of the id into some keeping with the outside
world. The passions of the id are modified by the sanity of
the ego in any ideal instance.[8] The super-ego, in Freud's
interpretation, represents the higher nature of man, originally associated with our fear and admiration of our parents.
These values later become incorporated in the super-ego or
"conscience," arising from the mastering of the Oedipus
complex.[9]

In Freud's view, then, the unconscious side of man con-
sists of the most socially undesirable aspects of his nature;
it contains the suppressed desires. There is, however, much

objection to Freud's interpretation of the unconscious. Joseph Jastrow, who calls Freud "exceptionally creative and as exceptionally uncritical,"[10] considers Freud's concept of the unconscious unnatural and unreliable, although he does see a good deal in Freud's general parallels between fantasying and daydreaming:[11] "The Freudian 'unconscious' is buried, but buried alive. The decease and funeral rites appear as suppression; the disturbing *revenant* in conflicts, fixations, complexes, perversions and what not — lively ghosts indeed, making a long continued Walpurgis of our supposedly dead selves on which we fail to rise to higher things, indeed rather descend to neurotic depths of misery and perversion. In such various ways has a false conception of the subconscious disastrous consequences for the understanding of the human make-up and set-up; and by that route it contributes to dubious, pernicious methods and false solutions for the direction of the intimate life."[12]

If Freud's picture of the unconscious part of man is not above reproach, what can we say of the remaining implications in his interpretation of the mind? Perhaps the most important fact to keep clearly before us is that Freud concerned himself with certain behaviours of the psychic apparatus of man, as he saw it, and drew his conclusions from his observations of this apparatus. As a result, our concept of man, it seems to me, now has been enlarged to contain not only the duality of body and soul, but the trilogy of body-psychic apparatus-soul.[13] Although psychology does not today concern itself with discussions of the soul, the psychic apparatus should not be confused with the soul, but, philosophically considered, may be regarded as an agent of the soul.[14] For instance in *Mind, Medicine, and Man,* Zilboorg cautiously places Freud's contribution in the main current of Western thought. According to Zilboorg, Freud's ideas do not contradict the basic philosophic concepts of St. Thomas Aquinas. Freud simply describes what he observes, without any attempt to account for the transformation of emotional drives or sense reactions into intellect and understanding. Freud does not argue against the "acting intellect" of St. Thomas, that part of man from which reason arises through forming abstractions. In fact, the inner images in which we abstract the outer world appear very similar in the thinking of both men, St. Thomas calling them "phantasmas" and Freud "representations."

Although we might try to recast Freudian psychology into Thomistic philosophy, feasible as the effort might be, it would only serve to show that men for centuries have been concerned with attempting to discover how man's perceptions are changed into thought or action. Philosophers of many varieties have struggled with the sharp division between body and soul, many attempts being made to find a common center where matter and spirit might meet. Freud's principal contribution, says Zilboorg, was his concept of a sort of psychic apparatus that partially helps to conceive of the continuity between the physiological and the mental. Freud's thinking thus tends to emphasize the dynamic experience of becoming human. If we relax the Freudian terminology, which after all is merely descriptive of what Freud believed might exist, we recognize the general nature of man as consisting of both unconscious and conscious motivations. Strictly speaking, Freudian psychoanalysis knows no more about the soul than theology knows about the Freudian psychic apparatus. One cannot be substituted for the other, although they may ultimately have some connection as yet unknown.[15]

Zilboorg thus gives us fair warning of attempting to make oversimple identifications between psychological and religious or philosophical terms and approaches. Psychology may lead us to the threshold of an understanding of man but cannot lead us beyond. As Thomas H. Hughes has indicated,[16] if we mistakenly choose to follow what are believed to be the implications of Freud, as many modern writers have, any concept of a spiritual reality is merely an illusion. These writers have not kept clearly separated, as Zilboorg insists we must, the "psychic apparatus" and the "soul." Otherwise we are left with the necessity of admitting that the idea of "God" results from the sex urge, which, through sublimation, achieves concepts of God as the father who protects, the ruler who rewards or punishes man's conduct, or finally as a lover who gives himself in love to satisfy deep emotional hunger and desire. The sex impulse would account for all religion, art, literature, and ethics through repression and its reappearance in a socially acceptable disguise. The sources of man's creative life, on the contrary, are not to be so easily explained away. Without creating the idealistic fallacy of saying that what "ought not to be is not," we still may agree that in the realm of religion both Freud and his disciples leave us dissatisfied.

Yet, remembering all of the limitations just suggested, we remind ourselves that it is still possible for serious critics to speak of the sources of creative effort in something of man's self beyond ordinary conscious control. In his *Poetry and Myth*, for instance, Frederick C. Prescott is firm in his belief that imaginative production cannot be confined to conscious effort. To do so would be to deal superficially with both the content and the form of imaginative art. Passing over the elements of art that may be due to conscious revision or deliberate thought, he says:

I am convinced that both the essential subject-matter and natural forms of poetry can be explained only by finding their origin in a visionary thought much more nearly related to our dreams than to our usual voluntary rational thought, to which critics tacitly if not openly are always trying to assimilate it. This visionary thought with the actuating emotion behind it, not only furnishes the poetic material, but obeying that "certain rhythm or order" of which Shelley speaks, by a vital law of its own shapes itself into those instinctive and primary forms in which all the forms consciously recognized by the poetic art originate. In other words the visionary thought is subjected to a control much more profound than can be exercised by a conscious art or a deliberate painstaking. Here lies the secret of Shakespeare's natural art, and upon such natural art all our "technique of the drama" is ultimately based. Aristotle's *Poetics* only records the instinctive habit of the Greek imagination.[17]

Perhaps at this point we would do well to recall some of Emerson's own statements on the subject of man's being. In highly metaphorical language he seems to be suggesting something of that reliance on the unconscious depths of life that Prescott sees as the ultimate source of genuine creative originality when he says in "The Poet": "As the traveler who has lost his way throws his reins on his horse's neck and trusts to the instinct of the animal to find his road, so must we do with the divine animal who carries us through this world."[18] In fact in all of his reliance on the intuitional self, Emerson devaluates the importance of the conscious part of the mind. Like Jones Very in his essay on Shakespeare,[19] Emerson sees the artist as ultimately passive; the basic, original materials of his art spring from the deeper sources of nature that flow through him.

Not only the subjects but the forms and vehicles of art likewise originate ultimately, Emerson believes, from the essential material and spiritual unity of the world. If we use the terminology of semantics, we may say that the language itself of poetry is in an Emersonian sense the "vehicle" of communication, while the spirit of nature gives the "tenor" to the expression. Emerson's ideal poet expresses universal insights; the deepest realities of nature communicate themselves through him as his intuitive self finds a voice in poetic images. To Emerson this was a cardinal conviction: "A man conversing in earnest, if he watch his intellectual processes, will find that a material image more or less luminous arises in his mind, contemporaneous with every thought, which furnishes the vestment of the thought. Hence, good writing and brilliant discourse are perpetual allegories. This imagery is spontaneous. It is the blending of experience with the present action of the mind. It is proper creation. It is the working of the Original Cause through the instruments he has already made."[20] In Emerson's theory his use of imagery is based on his psychological experiences of unpredictable moments of insight, giving hints of the unity of man and nature, seemingly whimsical in its revelations to man, as he mounts on "the stairway of surprise":[21] "Ah, not to me those dreams belong!/A better voice peals through my song."[22] This belief, of course, depends upon the confidence, expressed by Wordsworth in "The Recluse," that mind and matter are harmoniously adjusted to each other, as we recall:

> ...*my voice proclaims*
> *How exquisitely the Individual Mind*

*(And the progressive powers perhaps no less*
*Of the whole species) to the external World*
*Is fitted: — and how exquisitely, too —*
*Theme this but little heard of among men —*
*The external World is fitted to the Mind;*
*And the creation (by no lower name*
*Can it be called) which they will blended might*
*Accomplish: — this is our high argument.*[23]

As the world, including man himself, is the result of the creative energies of life, so the poem is the result of man's creative energies; or, more simply, the same creative force of life is manifested continuously in nature, man, and art. The same creative process is working in both nature and man.[24] In Emerson's belief, then, the idea and its expression could not be separated.

Let us look a bit more closely at this interpretation of the unconscious side of man's life. Speaking of the materials used by the mind, Emerson indicates something of the awareness that unexpected associations occur from experiences seemingly unnoticed. In "The American Scholar" he shows how present experience may later assume significance:

The actions and events of our childhood and youth are now matters of calmest observation. They lie like fair pictures in the air. Not so with our recent actions, — with the business which we now have in hand. On this we are quite unable to speculate. Our affections as yet circulate through it. We no more feel or know it than we feel the feet, or the hand, or the brain of our body. The new deed is yet a part of life, — remains for a time immersed in our unconscious life [that is, unnoticed because involved in present concerns]. In some contemplative hour it detaches itself from the life like a ripe fruit, to become a thought of the mind. Instantly it is raised, transfigured; the corruptible has put on incorruption. Henceforth it is an object of beauty, however base its origin and neighborhood. Observe too the impossibility of antedating this act. In its grub state, it cannot fly, it cannot shine, it is a dull grub. But suddenly, without observation, the selfsame thing unfurls beautiful wings, and is an angel of wisdom. So is there no fact, no event, in our private history, which shall not, sooner or later, lose its adhesive, inert form, and astonish us by soaring from our body into the empyrean.[25]

Of the workings of the unconscious aspect of the human being we have as yet little real knowledge. Modern psychology, however, most particularly in Jung and his followers, does not hesitate to place primary importance on the existence and function of man's unconscious. To summarize Jung's position in his *Psychology and Religion*,[26] for instance, the trend of much present thought is somewhat as follows: Human personality is composed of both conscious and unconscious aspects. The unconscious is immeasurably large; it is the submerged part of the iceberg, so to speak, much larger than the observable, conscious part. The consciousness to Jung is capable of being limited, but the unconsciousness is unlimited, or not capable of being limited, and thus not susceptible to definition. Despite the difficulty of describing the unconscious, we cannot avoid it because its results are found in the final productions known to the conscious mind. In short, fundamentally, Jung says, the unconsciousness is the undeveloped and unknown. We can really have no idea of what the unknown facts of the unconscious consist; we may observe their effects and assume they may be capable of being compared with the contents of the conscious in their psychical nature, but we cannot be positive. If such a similarity is admitted, however, we may say that human expression is the result not only of the contents of the conscious mind, related to the personal ego, but also issues from a sort of superordinated self in which the conscious ego is contained. This larger self is, scientifically speaking, indefinable, yet necessarily involved in any complete account of the psychic personality. According to Jung, the psyche often contains elements of superior insight, analysis, or knowledge that the conscious is incapable of producing. Such occurrences we call intuitive. But by giving man an intuition we have actually solved nothing because we must not overlook the fact that man does not make his intuition. An intuition, a hunch, as it is often called, comes to us. If we are quick enough, we pin it in its flight.

In Jung's interpretation, part of the materials stored in the unconscious originate in the individual's experience with the outside world as a result of his imaginative projection of himself, a process sometimes called "empathy" or "Einfühlung." Some identification of this sort appears essential if the world is not to seem a very empty place. According to Jung the world looks empty only to the man who does not know how to lead his energies outward toward objects and "render them alive and beautiful for himself, for Beauty does not indeed lie in things, but in the feeling that we give to them. That which compels us to create a substitute for ourselves is not the external lack of objects, but our incapacity to lovingly include a thing outside of ourselves."[27]

This, however, in Jung's thinking is not the whole story. He maintains that there is not only the personal conscious and unconscious but also what he calls a collective unconscious. The total interpretation is thus concerned with most recent object-images in the conscious, object-images from the person's own past that have been forgotten or ignored, but retained in the personal unconscious, and also general world-images inherited from the past of all humanity and retained in the collective unconscious.[28]

Now, the student of Emerson will have noted some degree of similarity between the thought of Jung and Emerson. Poets themselves recognize an unconscious aspect of the mind. Indeed, Prescott states in *The Poetic Mind*, "The poets certainly recognize the unconscious. Emerson's whole theory, for example, is based upon a recognition of it."[29] There is in poetic inspiration both a suddenness or spontaneity, which Emerson repeatedly refers to, and also an impersonal or superpersonal quality. These two characteristics Ribot regards as essential to the inspirational source of the creative imagination.[30]

The student of literature is, of course, under no compulsion to accept the theories or terminology of psychoanalysis, although it has influenced modern thought considerably. A question nevertheless remains for the reader of today who considers Emerson in the light of modern theories of the creative imagination. If the reader will allow a certain relaxing of psychoanalytic terminology, then, and will approach Emerson from a broadly human and esthetic point of view, he may consider that the origin of the creative imagination is in that aspect of the human psyche beyond conscious control — in that universal "spirit" familiar to Emerson's readers. Perhaps for the general reader Elisabeth Schneider best states the most unspecialized approach:

Imagination, then, as I understand it, is not a special or independent faculty: it is a particular way of bringing out into conscious use material from the unconscious or subconscious mind. In using these terms *unconscious* and *sub-*

*conscious* I do not mean to follow strictly the theory of the psychoanalytic school but only to postulate a human mind of many layers of operation, ranging indefinitely from most to least conscious. How far the degree of consciousness depends upon the phenomenon of attention and how far upon blocking or inhibiting or conflict is irrelevant to our purpose here.

But there are two more or less distinguishable ways in which we bring to conscious use that which had been unconscious. One is primarily logical and analytical; the other is not. It is this other non-logical way that we call imaginative. We seem to have the power of *subjecting this material to our attention,* and yet at the same time of *allowing it to remain free of the mind's rational control.* Why or how this occurs, and why the power to do it varies from time to time and from person to person, we do not know.[31]

We may say, then, that originality arises from the creative work of the unconscious. In this sense, originality is nature itself working with freedom and spontaneity beyond personal control: "Not from a vain and shallow thought/His awful Jove young Phidias brought."[32] Intentional thought is superficial compared with the unconscious faculty, the more vital part of the mind of which the conscious is a special tool.[33] The poet relies ultimately on uncontrolled, associative thought whenever he is confronted with the really difficult subjects of life.[34]

Emerson's favorite subjects are those generally most difficult of definition: beauty, truth, goodness, soul, immortality, nature, and the like. If both he and present thinkers broadly agree in the unconscious sources of life, what major distinctions must the modern reader make between Emerson and a psychologist like Jung?

The outstanding differences, as I see them, are in Emerson's interpretation of the content of the deeper aspects of man's spirit and in his attitude toward the images or symbols of imaginative projection.

As readers of William James' *Varieties of Religious Experience* will recall, James saw Emerson as an essentially healthy spirit; his life is well balanced and adjusted to the world. If depressions of spirit occur, he rather quickly recovers. It can hardly be doubted that what seems to some readers as unusual optimism in Emerson arises significantly out of his belief in an ultimately favorable relationship between man and his world. Although Emerson could say, " '... if I am the Devil's child, I will live then from the Devil' "[35] in following the intuitions of his own nature, the inescapable impression from what he has chosen to project of himself in his poetry is that of a life remarkably free of emotional stress and strain. It seems to me this projection could hardly have occurred without an ultimate harmony of Emerson's own psychological self. To Emerson the world appeared a spiritual unity. The flowing of the river Musketaquid, the waves of the sea, the varied fortunes and personalities of men indicated to him an essential unity of life. Man's self had a universal referent. To rely on one's self was to rely on the potentialities of the universe, for man's life, rightly understood, represented an epitome or a microcosm of all life, just as a drop of water may tell us all there is to know about the ocean. For Emerson, then, the total self is an active, harmonious whole; the deepest reach of man's self is not repressed, as Freud believes, or merely undeveloped, as Jung believes. In Emerson's own words: "Man is conscious of a universal soul within or behind his individual life, wherein, as in a firmament, the natures of

Justice, Truth, Love, Freedom, arise and shine. This universal soul he calls Reason: it is not mine, or thine, or his, but we are its; we are its property and men. And the blue sky in which the private earth is buried, the sky with its eternal calm, and full of everlasting orbs, is the type of Reason. That which intellectually considered we call Reason, considered in relation to nature, we call Spirit. Spirit is the Creator. Spirit hath life in itself."[36]

In the second place, in his attitude toward images, Emerson scarcely follows the path of Jung. We might be tempted to believe so from such a passage as that in "The Poet" where Emerson advances the belief that "poetry was all written before time was, and whenever we are so finely organized that we can penetrate into that region where the air is music, we hear those primal warblings and attempt to write them down, but we lose ever and anon a word or a verse and substitute something of our own, and thus miswrite the poem."[37]

But we must recall that as an introspective poet placing the very highest value on imagination, Emerson was always likely to be dissatisfied with the final poetic product. Emerson could hardly have believed in a common reservoir of archetypal images, it seems to me, because he repeatedly emphasizes that not only is nature constantly a very fluid symbol for individual interpretation but also the individual mind or spirit of man re-creates nature itself. For instance in a passage from an unpublished lecture, "The Poet," Emerson maintains that the mind finds unlimited prospects in nature: "The sense of nature is inexhaustible. You think you know the meaning of these tropes of nature, and to-day you come into a new thought, and lo! all nature converts itself into a symbol of that, and you see it has been chanting that song like a cricket ever since the creation.... 'T was the moral of the river, the rock and the ocean. The river, the rock and the ocean say 'Guess again.' "[38] In Emerson's interpretation, nature is not a fixed, static referent, although to the unimaginative it may often appear to be, but a fluid expression of a dynamic creative spirit. One of Emerson's most serious criticisms of Swedenborg, for instance, was in his rigid set of symbols based on nature and his narrow interpretation of the Scriptures.[39] The "mystic," like Swedenborg, may have a mind closed against the active creative energies of the universe that made life dynamic and experimental for Emerson. Edward Waldo Emerson clearly records this attitude of his father when he wrote of his walks in the woods in *Emerson in Concord:* "He daily went out from the four walls of his study to his larger study in the woods, recorded what he saw, but largely, not as a final fact, — as it were, with a pin through it, — but as an appearance, a suggestion, a parable, surely with wisdom behind it. He saw light, flowers, shadow on solid rock, but what he noted was, that the light glanced, the flower unfolded, the shadow passed, and even the rock was crumbling under the tooth of the air to pass into soil, then flower, then seed, then man: that all was flowing and new each moment."[40] In allowing nature to speak through him the poet receives expressions from central creative energies of life, as it were, already partly revealed in organic relationships of nature; but, from this source, the creative self of man may project a further creation so that the poem "adorns nature with a new thing."[41] The imaginative spirit of man continues the creative work of nature: "All the facts of the animal economy, sex, nutriment, gestation, birth, growth, are symbols of the passage of the world into the soul of man, to suffer

there a change and reappear a new and higher fact."[42]
Emerson does not follow Jung's farfetched assumption of a
"collective unconscious." In this way he coincides with
modern critics of Jung who regard this concept as highly
questionable if not impossible.[43]

Admittedly it is very unlikely that the critic can ever
state with certainty what materials of the final version of
a literary work were due to "unconscious" or "conscious"
sources since it is hardly possible for the writer himself to
state what was entirely working in his mind when he wrote
a certain line or used a certain image. The total created
fabric of a poem is a complex interweaving of multiple
factors with which conscious attention and modification
may have more or less to do.[44] Every student of Emerson
knows he was not a careless poet: he often considerably
revised the original drafts of his poems, the final versions
not being published until years afterward. It has been shown,
for instance, that Emerson's "Terminus" was probably first
written at a time when he was deeply disturbed by the
political and moral aspects of slavery; it was later modified
and adapted to refer primarily to approaching old age.[45]
Further bibliographical investigations of Emerson's manuscripts may reveal more about the integration of varied
experiences that Emerson achieved.

If "Terminus" may be taken as an example of the highly
revised poem, "Days" and "Seashore" may represent lesser
degrees of revision, coming closer, in our sense, to the "unconscious" source of poetic imagination. In them perhaps
the artist's underlying "wish" is least controlled by his more
apparent artistic "intent." Speaking of the composition of
"Days," Emerson said: "I find one state of mind does not
remember or conceive of another state. Thus I have written

within a twelvemonth verses ('Days') which I do not remember the composition or correction of, and could not
write the like to-day, and have only, for proof of their
being mine, various external evidences, as the manuscripts
in which I find them, and the circumstance that I have sent
copies of them to friends, etc. Well, if they had been better,
if it had been a noble poem, perhaps it would have only
more entirely taken up the ladder into heaven."[46] Perhaps
partly because he considered this poem as largely "given"
him from more than ordinary conscious sources, Emerson,
as his son tells us, once said that "Days" was perhaps his
best poem.[47] We also have Emerson's account of the origin
of "Seashore." Emerson had taken his family in July, 1857,
to spend two weeks at Pigeon Cove, on Cape Ann. On the
day after their return to Concord, Emerson, his son recalls,
came to read a passage from his journal to the family in
their mother's room, where they were all sitting. Emerson
said, "I came in yesterday from walking on the rocks and
wrote down what the sea had said to me; and to-day, when
I open my book, I find it all reads as blank verse, with
scarcely a change."[48] The passage he then read contains the
majority of the images as well as the general rhythmic flow
of two-thirds of the poem, to which he added closing lines.

It can hardly be doubted, then, that Emerson's creative
imagination furnished unawares both images and rhythms
that appear in the published work. The creative energies
seem to have intrinsic pulses as well as concrete projections
in images, or, perhaps rather, the images are propelled by
the rhythmical impulses of the creative activity. These impulses, I would say, account largely for poetic invention
and individuality; the control of these impulses results in
more regularized or traditional form and is thus more

"social." As readers of poetry know, there are many gradations between the most unconventional and the most traditional in poetic forms and styles.[49] These adjustments between extremes may be discovered by comparing, for instance, Shelley or Whitman with Pope or Tennyson. In theory, nevertheless, we need to recall, Emerson believes that every creation reflects the organic, unified life energies, which at the outset may be beyond conscious control. This unconscious side of creation appears to be visionary or dreamlike in its unpredictability. Emerson regards the poet as a seer, and he even uses an image associated with dreaming when he admits the depths of the creative life: "Poppy leaves are strewn when a generalization is made, for I can never remember the circumstances to which I owe it, so as to repeat the experiment or put myself in the conditions."[50] Precisely how unconscious and conscious invention are linked is still a mystery; probably the simplest generalization that can be made is that the intellectual or emotional processes involved in unconscious development are not fully reducible to conscious understanding because the preparatory work is unnoticed and thus enters the conscious fully made.[51] These intellectual and emotional processes may not be inimical to conscious modes of composition but merely, as it were, undiscovered — the uncharted seas.

While I believe the general tendency of Freud to emphasize neurotic repressions among emotional sources of imaginative projections is inadequate for understanding Emerson, both Freud and Jung suggest that human consciousness is in some way, as yet not fully understood, connected with the process of forming analogies from the outside world and coming into contact with verbal images, memory-residues that at first were perceptions derived primarily from auditory perceptions, the visual components of which are derived from reading.[52] We are reminded here of the broad parallel in Emerson's thinking when he repeatedly states the significance of language and metaphor: "Every word was once a poem. Every new relation is a new word."[53] He sees the poet as the language-maker, bringing into conscious communication the deepest insights of life. "This insight, which expresses itself by what is called Imagination, is a very high sort of seeing, which does not come by study, but by the intellect being where and what it sees; by sharing the path or circuit of things through forms, and so making them translucid to others."[54] One of the mind's greatest abilities is the tendency of its images as they freely play to become metaphorical; they become our "primitive abstractions," the "spontaneous embodiments of general ideas."[55]

The artist, of course, is limited by the materials he uses. The sculptor is limited by the kind of marble he chooses, the poet by his words and images. Revision may be determined by the interplay of the original materials consciously observed and to some extent redirected. Indeed the final conception of a poem may not come until it has been executed; that is, the full process must occur before the final "intent" may actually be realized. Occupied by his subject matter, the writer's interest suggests conscious refinements or revisions. The material itself, once originating in the ideas and emotions of the writer, tends to fertilize his creative efforts further while he is rewording them.[56] A straightforward expression is seldom an expression at all when we are trying to suggest intrinsic qualities of a vividly moving creative thought. In the attempt to be more accurate the poet may actually make his work more complex. That is to say that complexity need not always arise from the seeming waywardness of the unconsciously given materials but also may result from the intention of the artist to convey more particularly the peculiar or individual qualities of the experience as he sees it. Language, being a social instrument, if it is too commonly used by the imaginative artist, may actually defeat the very expression he was motivated to convey. Dissatisfied with what he consciously observes as the materials of his expression, the artist may attempt to invent more precise metaphors that will more completely arouse the particular quality of response on which his interests are centered. In this sense we must partially modify the belief that the original "inspired" material is the only "original" thing in a poem; part of what makes a poem a new thing may be due to the diligent revision of the conscious mind. In the opinion of the artist the materials first coming to him, valuable and fundamental as they may be, may nevertheless appear not altogether final to his conscious intent of trying to be accurate in suggesting the more subtle qualities of the experience, which may have become the most stirring or significant to him.[57]

In all these considerations there is, however, a final point that I believe has central bearing on the interpretation that the modern mind can place on Emerson's poetry. Whether or not we are disposed to consider the validity of any spiritual reality beyond the total "psychological" self, it is inescapable that Emerson gives us the impression that there is a spiritual reality in all life kindred to what he experienced within himself. Perhaps this belief was only an imaginative projection of himself on to the outside world in an attempt to make life harmonious, humane, benevolent, or what one will. The fact remains that the ultimate reality to Emerson was an essential unity of life, both physically and spiritually. In this belief of his, we discover, it seems to me, the secret of the unified spirit of his poetry. In judging his writing it is important not only to remember the possible unity that I have tried to suggest he may have achieved between the basic materials arising from the unconscious and the finally revised materials from the conscious, but also to reflect that, as we see from Zilboorg's interpretation of Freud, no matter what the uncharted reaches of the unconscious apparatus may be, there is still the possibility of a further extent of man's being, carrying us into what has usually been called the "soul." This is the final step, precarious as it may be, that we must take in explaining some of the ways of the imagination as disclosed in the works of Emerson. While much literature may doubtless be written to appeal to the reader because, as Hanns Sachs says, the writer wishes to obtain the relief of his guilt feeling and, inseparable from this, the replacement of his narcissism by devoting extra attention to the style and form of his poem, there is more to literature than a desire to make us all brothers in sin. In some kinds of literature this appeal becomes unnecessary. In what we may call "religious" art the emotional stimulation of individuals is not primary, if present at all. The faith in an ultimate spiritual reality entirely replaces the authority of the "super-ego" of Freud's apparatus. Any conflicts and repressions, if there, are thrown entirely into the background. The appeal is not of excitement and passion but of final harmony and serenity. The individual is almost lost in this impersonal art.[58] The materials of his art are not used to stimulate the reader's participation in private eccentricities but to free him from individual tumult to participate imaginatively, spiritually in a universal harmony. An essential quality of Emerson's poetic art may therefore be called religious by his own definition: "Religion or worship is the attitude of those who see this unity, intimacy and sincerity; who see that against all appearances the nature of things works for truth and right forever."[59]

A modern psychologist need no more rule out the possibility of the soul of man than did the nineteenth-century Sampson Reed, with whom this chapter began. I do not wish to cavil over this point. If anyone does not prefer to give at any time the creative products of man what he may regard as perhaps an unreasonably vague and a possibly undesirable "metaphysical" origin, but sees all types of imaginative achievement originating at most from unconscious mental activity, he of course is privileged to do so. Even if one prefers to go no further than the broad unconscious aspect of the creative mind, without any "supernatural" coloring, he will at least recall that to Emerson as to other poets the mysterious depths of the mind were not inferior and foul. As Lionel Trilling reminds us, "The hidden element takes many forms and it is not always 'dark' and 'bad'; for Blake, Wordsworth and Coleridge what was hidden and unconscious was wisdom and power, working even in despite of the conscious intellect, and for Matthew Arnold the mind was fed by streams buried deeper than we can know."[60]

Also, to Emerson at all events, the world outside man — "nature" — is "good" because it has values for the mind and spirit. Rightly understood, the world, Emerson believed, presents a panorama of related examples of the evolution of life in its unconscious drive and experimental strivings to become man. Only man himself can fully appreciate this result since he alone is actually conscious of it, just as within himself he realizes there are unconscious creative energies, which he cannot fully understand but can highly value. Emerson's view of the creative evolution of life forms a consistent whole. As creative processes in literature are based on spontaneous, unconscious "inspirations" of the poet, so, in present terminology, "Emerson's evolutionism would be described as mutational. He did not believe that evolution takes place by the gradual accumulation of minute variations, but by comparatively sudden jumps as the individual fulfills a need, or, in the language of 'Fate,' as Power accommodates itself to or triumphs over Circumstance."[61] Progress is achieved by sudden transformations, not by slow accumulations. This general attitude serves to illustrate broadly Emerson's belief in the unpredictable appearance of the superior individual who may himself transform the history of mankind as well as the appearance of the transforming power of poetic inspiration. As a man of optimistic faith, Emerson accepted evolution fearlessly.[62] To him nature at large repeats the same ethical and creative purposes found in humanity. The emphasis on the ultimate goodness of life found in progressive evolution would enable Emerson to believe that through mutation the ethics of Christ, for instance, represent a moral achievement of life appearing unpredictably on the human scene. But, being an idealist, Emerson saw truths constantly in nature. "The world proceeds from the same spirit as the body of man. It is a remoter and inferior incarnation of God, a projection of God in the unconscious."[63]

As a reflective poet, looking inward, Emerson reveals in his imaginative projections an introvertive preference for the "idea" side of the image; he removes in varying degrees the more physical aspects of the image so that the pure gold of abstraction will be free of the alloy of the concrete. He tends to see the ideal "thought" within nature or within the image.[64] Emerson thus sees that through his inmost intuitions and impulses man becomes one with the living spirit of all life. Man, as the highest reach of life, may use matter plastically, shaping it through his mind to realize itself more completely.[65] A careful reader of Emerson will have noted that he seldom personifies "God." He finds the creative spiritual essence within man's mind. "He makes a sharp distinction between the intellect, that is the mind operative in ordinary conscious thought, with the will that guides it, and the 'over-soul,' which certainly includes, if it is not identical with, the unconscious mind in question."[66] As I have indicated, it may be preferable to distinguish between the concept of the unconscious apparatus of the mind and the concept of the soul; but we might at least hazard the suggestion that in their application to Emerson the two indeed seem to blend into each other in the deepest reaches of man's being. Linking man with unconscious external nature, in Emerson's view, the "unconscious" in man remains as a sort of instrumental extension of the soul, the two partially uniting in their intimate creative work animated by the soul, which only in man has achieved some awareness of its presence. The "soul" may include, then, something of the "unconscious" — or rather it would seem working through the "unconscious" — but may not, as I see it, be limited to what psychoanalysis usually calls the unconscious.[67] Without wishing to deal in wearisome distinctions, however, we may indeed regard Emerson's "God" as a sort of mythic projection of the mind itself. As Prescott says, "If to God all desires are known and from him no secrets are hid, it is because this externalization represents not only the conscious but the unconscious portions of the mind."[68] Emerson's "over-soul" is probably in fact the "indwelling soul."

Finally, no one who has taken pains to appreciate the essential Freud will have missed the point that, after all, Freud's concept of the human being is a creature of love, not aggression.[69] If we are willing to take the step that Freud did not, it may be possible at least to suggest without gross exaggeration that, if we consider the possibility of participating in life by projecting one's love outwardly to attempt to achieve that happiest state of loving and being loved[70] and, in this sense, surrender to a power at once deeper and larger than the limited conscious self, man might humbly and serenely discover in himself the benevolent, creative spirit of life that to Emerson was God.[71]

# CHAPTER III

## *The Organic Language of Poetry*

### 1

ONE OF THE PRINCIPAL ATTRACTIONS of poetry is the psychological appeal that imagery can make to the sensitive reader. This fact is especially significant in a study of Emerson's poetry, where we are dealing with a writer whose momentary insights, projected through varied associations, were of paramount importance to him. As William James remarked, "The form of the garment was so vital with Emerson that it is impossible to separate it from the matter. They form a chemical combination — thoughts which would be trivial expressed otherwise, are important through the nouns and verbs to which he married them. The style is the man, it has been said; the man Emerson's mission culminated in his style, and if we must define him in one word, we have to call him Artist. He was an artist whose medium was verbal and who wrought in spiritual material."[1] Studying images, then, is more than enjoying decoration or listing rhetorical devices. This generalization is basic not only because of the exalted value Emerson placed on the poet as language-maker[2] but also because of the very texture of language itself; the study of symbolic thought is constantly challenging. In a concluding passage of her *Philosophy in a New Key*, Susanne K. Langer makes this point very clear: "Sign

42

and symbol are knotted together in the production of those fixed realities that we call 'facts,' as I think this whole study of semantics has shown. But *between the facts* run the threads of unrecorded reality, momentarily recognized, wherever they come to the surface, in our tacit adaptation to signs; and the bright, twisted threads of symbolic envisagement, imagination, thought — memory and reconstructed memory, belief beyond experience, dream, make-believe, hypothesis, philosophy — the whole creative process of ideation, metaphor, and abstraction that makes human life an adventure in understanding."[3] Style is more than a medium; it is thought itself.[4] As we have seen, Emerson trusted his intuitive thought; some of his best poems, like "Days" and "Seashore," seem to have come to him spontaneously.

It is a psychological fact, of course, that the world shapes the mind of the writer; we need only recall in this instance how thoroughly the New England countryside penetrated Emerson's thinking. It is equally clear, however, that the truly creative writer adds something new to this world as he may mold it closer to his heart's desire. The world passes through the magic alembic of the poet's mind to become a distillation of fresh meaning and beauty.[5] Readers of Emerson's poetry may think of a number of examples of his imaginative originality in this respect; the poet can say even of the industrial towns and cities that "They are but sailing foam-bells/Along Thought's causing stream."[6] There will of course be various levels of imagery according to the quality of imagination active at the moment. It seems to me that a poet's success can be measured rather largely by the degree to which he at least momentarily causes his reader to believe in the validity of the poetic image. In this sense the greatest poets are those who so completely realize the significance of the image employed as to make the word one with the thing.

Although the philosophic tone is dominant in Emerson's poetry, to attempt to paraphrase poetic thought may seem either unjust or irrelevant if not downright murderous to the body of poetry.[7] But, as I see it, the paraphrase can do little harm if the critic only frankly states the suggestions he has received as he follows the whole communication closely and also if critics generally do not become entangled in discussions of controversial social, moral, or philosophic points that themselves in paraphrase probably only remotely suggest what the poet himself had in mind. It may be finally useless to try to determine the more subtle, fine points of a poet's work. At the same time, it is inevitable that any work may have associations of which the poet himself was unaware; every reader will read a poem in his own way.[8] Yet, in all fairness to the poet — or to his poem — we must try to read his expression in the best light of his work as a whole. The entire process is thus a delicate adjustment between the poet's effort to communicate and the reader's effort to understand, and the interplay is beyond neat confines, as I. A. Richards has shown in *Science and Poetry*.[9] Aroused by his interests, the words of the poet present themselves to his consciousness in a form that serves to order his experience. It is "the tide of impulses," in Richards' phrase, that is the source of the words. Sweeping through the poet's mind, these words represent the experience itself, not comments about it. They in turn stir the reader, who participates in reverse in the experience. From the poet's words, combinations of impulses are aroused within the reader. The words of the poet are thus genuine keys; they unlock for the reader something of the character of the poet's mind in so far as we can judge by what the poet has chosen to reveal as he allows us to see life from his angle of vision, as he projects himself in the words he has finally chosen to use.

To examine a poet's creative use of language may be a somewhat rigorous journey, but perhaps the sympathetic reader may find that the port is, in Emerson's words, "well worth the cruise."[10] As we study the tendency of Emerson's poetic expression through images we become increasingly aware of the Emersonian approach as we respond to the interwoven image-ideas from the fabric of the poetry representing Emerson's unified imaginative vision of life. These strands of images disclose the very life of the Emersonian myth as it weaves its fascinating web. We see Emerson driven by the controlling interest of his imaginative life to create a core of belief while, at the same time, the associative faculties of his mind are allowed to run free.

2

From an attentive reading of Emerson's poetry, what do we gather about the general tone of his mind as revealed through the images, giving keys to the tendency of his thought? His poetry contains a fairly wide range of subjects in its images. Here let us indicate the principal tendencies of his imaginative approach to life as suggested by the associations through which it is conveyed.

In the first place, a systematic investigation of Emerson's poetic matrix shows that his interpretation of the arts is consistently intellectual. For instance, his images based on art, like those in "The Snow-Storm," indicate that Emerson thought at times of both nature and man's life in terms of the mason or architect as well as the sculptor. It was, however, not essentially esthetic values that attracted him to architecture and sculpture but rather the intellectual associations with them from which he could draw moral or philosophic parallels in his imagery. Likewise images from painting in a poem like "Monadnoc" or "May-Day" are apparently more generalized than those from either architecture or sculpture not simply because Emerson did not have a particularly good eye for painting but because he probably found less opportunity in painting to illustrate his philosophic and ethical ideas.

Emerson's imagery referring to music is also notably concerned with philosophic concepts of nature or poetry. Although Emerson makes a good deal of the music of nature, he seldom is content to give us a musical impression for its own sake; he must read a philosophic suggestion into it. This tendency helps intensify the characteristic intellectual cast of the imagery. Emerson tells us in "Merlin," for example, that our minds may be entranced on occasion by the constant harmonies and rhythms of nature until the contrapuntal melodies and regular beat of morning and evening fill us with a kind of spiritual intoxication, "As the two twilights of the day/Fold us music-drunken in."[11] To Emerson beauty in the fine arts offers an avenue to reach moral values or spiritual truths.

When we consider Emerson's images of theological associations, in our attempt to trace the emerging pattern of his imaginative attitudes, we find that his thought remains free from conventional theology to a large extent; his spiritual truths, as we might expect, do not depend on any dogma. Yet scattered through his poetry are images depending on religious personages or ideas, like Adam, Daniel, Pentecost, and the star of Bethlehem, and reflecting his early training in the Christian ministry. Emerson imaginatively used Biblical materials in clusters of images conveying his own independent approach to the spiritual life. We continue to see how his imagination constructs in his personal myth a set of values consistently valid for the self from which they rise. Emerson succeeds in giving, as an imaginative artist, a fresh luster to the old religious lore. The traditional knowledge of Christian folk now becomes blended with his personal wisdom.

From the science of his day Emerson also extracts through imaginative associations elements contributing to his individual attitudes. His spiritual assurance allows no essential conflict between science and religion such as troubled Tennyson and Arnold. His spiritually bulwarked imagination freely uses scientific data whenever they assist personal insights. Emerson used both Christian religion and contemporary science transcendentally for his own philosophic concept of the imaginative life. The idea of the atom, for instance, had a special hold on his imagination, for he uses it in various ways to illustrate his thinking about man and nature. The image of the spiral or of the circle also gave hints to his imagination of the evolving, yet unified, movement of living processes. In fact some of his most eloquent lines, like those in "Woodnotes II," disclose for us his poetic version of evolution in their subjective interpretation of current scientific thought. Science, to Emerson, presented a source of truths not rigidly limited to factual analysis but broadly suggestive of imaginative experience. In short, Emerson believed that unless science can be used imaginatively it ceases to exist as humane knowledge.

Emerson as mythmaker especially becomes clear when we study the ways his imagination follows in its associations with some of the mythological patterns of earlier cultures. We can sense something of his need for building a set of personal beliefs concerning the spiritual quality of life. "Fortune, Minerva, Muse, Holy Ghost, — these are quaint names, too narrow to cover this unbounded substance."[12] From the mass of mythological lore Emerson's imaginative needs draw varied elements, reshaped into something of a new order. Through this selection of materials from collective mythology, a kind of individual myth is re-created. Emerson's freedom of imaginative treatment, already traced through his interpretation of art, religion, and science, shows particular power in his broad blending of mythological subjects. Unlike Milton, however, Emerson was not a highly conscious reconstructor of mythic pattern. But his free use of mythology intensifies our impressions of his search for a new order of values.

The significant fact, it seems to me, about the appearance of mythological materials in Emerson's poetry is not that he may have distorted somewhat the original subjects but that he introduces them with imaginative discrimination resulting in an aura of romance. Indeed, Jove, Bacchus, and Cupid as they appear in Emerson's poetry may hardly be what they were to the ancients because his imagination has transformed them into symbolic representations at once more personal but perhaps broader in implication. The figure of Jove as the symbol of intellectual superiority, of Bacchus as the bringer of spiritual ecstasy, and of Cupid as the initiator in love have an essential unity since to Emerson's mind they become imaginative manifestations of aspects of the universal spirit underlying all life. There could be no incongruity to him because the laws of his own spirit appeared to him the laws of all spirits; they were part of the all-pervading mind. Emerson's portrayal of Pan, then, represents an inevitable rereading of an old mythological figure in a new interpretation. To nineteenth-century Emerson, Pan suggests a particular version of the All, a life force that to him symbolizes evolutionary mutations from unconscious nature to the finally conscious man, aware of spontaneous spiritual growth. In this light it seems to me beside the point to say, for instance, that Emerson is not a good Greek; he was not trying to be. Imaginative uses of mythological materials occur since by blending ancient subjects with his own thinking he achieved the degree of originality that interested him.

The awesome spiritual assurance of Uriel perhaps projects Emerson in one of his most effective moments as myth-maker. It is worth noting, however, that the intellectual dominance of Jove appealed to him, but he made little of the daring vigor of Prometheus, who played so central a part in the imagination of the Shelley of "Prometheus Unbound." Emerson's spiritual faith probably led him to believe difficulties could be overcome too easily to appreciate fully the struggle of Prometheus and the inherent tragedy in the ever-present possibility of man's losing his battle for freedom.

Nowhere in his poetry do we find reflections of the Anglo-Saxon imagination like Beowulf and Grendel. Unlike Longfellow, he does not write about the mighty Norse gods. On the other hand, a somewhat esoteric romanticism is suggested in his symbolic use of the Sphinx, associated with the mystery and glamour of ancient Egypt.

Emerson's use of the semimythological Merlin from the Arthurian legends becomes all the more striking when we consider that he makes no mention of Lancelot and Guine-

vere or of the Holy Grail. His temperamental reserve toward the emotion of love, analyzed with typical intellectuality in "Give All to Love" and "To Rhea," probably
prevented him from feeling the conflict between spirit and
flesh in the passionate love drama of Lancelot and Guinevere.
The long search for the Holy Grail and Lancelot's final re-
nunciation of the world could have held little meaning for
Emerson, who, living so completely a life of serene, unques-
tioning faith, felt that heaven must exist, if anywhere, within
man in a sort of eternal present.

At all events, Emerson seems to have been interested
in varied traditional mythologies, where he found enough
points of imaginative sympathy to cause him to adapt mythological figures to his own philosophy of man's divinity.
Emerson thought in terms of a broad mythological imagery
that resulted in giving sweep and expanse to his poetry and
at the same time in making it possible to condense his ideas
neatly in a set of concrete images.

Further evidence of Emerson's subjective approach to
life arises from considering his poetic images from history
and literature. Their slightness indicates his want of interest
in these subjects. As an introspective philosopher Emerson
believed that whatever history or literature could tell us of
man already existed in the imaginative possibilities of his
own mind. Emerson speaks as a truly assured mythmaker
when he announces in his introductory poem to the essay
"History":

> *I am owner of the sphere,*
> *Of the seven stars and the solar year,*
> *Of Caesar's hand, and Plato's brain,*
> *Of Lord Christ's heart, and Shakspeare's strain.*[13]

Images reflecting associations with systematic philosophy

are also rare in Emerson's poems. He uses philosophic suggestions to suit his own imaginative purposes. Although he read rather widely in philosophy, he preferred to find his truths in the solitude of his spirit.

Even if literary references are slight in Emerson's poetic images, he found ways of giving a mythic significance to events of daily life as an important element in his own poetic matrix. Emerson significantly uses familiar materials from common experience. We soon realize his characteristic intellectuality when he treats everyday subjects. Unlike Keats, Emerson has an imagination that stimulates little sensuous perception. We miss imagery appealing to our senses. Emerson's intellectualized imagination has removed the basic physical qualities from his materials. He conforms to his mythic pattern when he says for instance in "Merlin" that "Flavor gladly blends with flavor"[14] instead of giving us an immediate sensuous perception of the fact. The idea of the blending of flavors is more important to Emerson than the flavors themselves. Again, Emerson usually introduces images of jewels for a philosophic purpose; he presents hardly any sense of the glitter or brilliance of jewelry, although suggestions of rubies and opals add some color to these images. On the other hand, perhaps one of the most significant images in all of Emerson's poetry is that of wine, used as it is in "Bacchus" and "Woodnotes II" to suggest his concept of man's spiritual intoxication by the world-soul.

In general it appears that by tracing the evidence of materials from everyday life in Emerson's poems we further realize his success in projecting his mythic vision. His philosophy is sometimes strikingly expressed through sharp images recalling his couplet in which he gives an estimate of his imaginative powers: "I have an arrow that will find its mark,/A mastiff that will bite without a bark."[15] His imaginative trend of mind enhances commonplace materials as he follows his own advice: "Give to barrows, trays and pans,/Grace and glimmer of romance."[16]

In comparison with the imaginative treatment of associations with daily life, images from military life show us that Emerson was interested in using references to rifles, cannons, bullets, banners, or tents to convey imaginatively phases of man's personality or pictures of nature. Large battle scenes, as we might expect, are missing; we are removed from the clash and clamor of war. But there does emerge, nevertheless, Emerson's ideal of the intellectually dominant hero who not only meets his duty on the battlefield but through spiritual discipline conquers in the even greater struggles for peace.

This view of the essential spiritual nobility of the human being motivates the final choice of images referring to the human body and personality. Although we realize that Emerson loved humanity, there remain in him a shyness and an aloofness that prevent his poetry from reaching anything like the rich emotional quality of a Shakespeare. Emerson in this respect differs markedly from Whitman, whose poems are often permeated with a sense of physical presence and warm affection. Just as in Emerson's images from daily life we miss the sensuousness of a Keats, in the images based on the physical aspects of human life we feel continually that Emerson's philosophic cast of mind is preventing him from realizing in his images the immediate impact of human feeling. Such images are diluted, on the whole, by his mental preferences until much of the emotional or sensuous potentiality of the material has disappeared. Here again, of course, we have evidence of the subjectiveness noted repeatedly throughout Emerson's poetry, addressing the mind primarily. Although emotional qualities can be found in the imagery, its prevailing tone is imparted by Emerson's philosophic imagination. Probably this want of human immediacy may always prevent Emerson from becoming a popular poet.

For many readers, however, Emerson's poetry may be redeemed through the grace of its imaginative view of nature. In his poems there is a considerable body of personifications of aspects of nature and of abstractions from human life that I think continue to indicate the subjective approach to materials that we have noted in other connections. We find personifications of the mountain, sea, river, forest, flowers, birds, and insects. Even the day, the seasons, and time itself are personified. These images further reveal Emerson's mythmaking faculty in his endowing parts of nature with human qualities.

Although Emerson's imagination appears to be working at a high level of intensity when he brings nature close to his reader by fusing human values with natural phenomena, the life of man seems quite far removed when Emerson is indulging in his fondness for intellectual abstractions of life. Instead of being able to portray characters in revealing situations, as, for instance, Browning did in his dramatic monologues, Emerson must be content to personify abstractions from life in slender allegories. The style of most of the passages employing abstractions and personifications reminds us of eighteenth-century neoclassical poetry. However, I do not think that, on the whole, any possible literary influence has special significance in this study of Emerson's imagery. Whatever general parallels may exist between his imagery and that of neoclassical poetry can be explained largely by the coincidence that in this particular at least his instincts for style were working in the same channel as those of a typical neoclassical poet. His intellectuality caused him to think in abstract terms, however far removed his intuitive faith may ultimately be from the rationalism of neoclassic thought. On the other hand, Emerson's farfetched wit can be found in his frequent use of the metaphysical conceit, which helps bring the tone of some of his imagery close to that of a seventeenth-century writer like Herbert.

In his "Song of Nature" Emerson has Nature say that "Time and Thought were my surveyors,/They laid their courses well."[17] From Emerson's work as a whole we know, of course, that there can be no philosophic distinction between the basic creative activity of this "Thought" in nature and in man. If we would put Emerson's central approach in a word, it is this "Thought" that unifies everything he wrote. It has been, broadly speaking, the controlling factor determining his use of imagery. It accounts for his reading himself into the images from mythology, his free interpretation of Christian religion, the philosophic reading of images from art and music, his subjective approach to science, his cavalier neglect of history, his admiration for the intellectually powerful hero in war or peace, the want of sensuousness in his images from daily life, and his reticence in dealing with the human body. In short, our study of Emerson's imagery has confirmed our impression that it was a characteristic intellectuality that everywhere operated uppermost in his choice and use of images. While this approach constitutes an obvious limitation for any poet, it is in this very subjective quality, placing the individual as the measure of all, that, if it limits the appeal of the poems, gives them their undoubted stamp of creative originality. Whatever beauty this poetry possesses must come from the innate character of Emerson's own mind. Refashioned through his intuitive imagination, life becomes in its projection of his values and beliefs a composite Emersonian myth.

Largely because the correspondences between aspects of nature suggested to Emerson's imagination the consequent unity he believed must prevail between a natural fact and a law of the mind or spirit, the idea of natural relationships was one of his favorite concepts. Some of his most attractive images illustrate this sort of unity among natural objects. The relationships suggested appear to be mainly intuitional; they are least touched by his desire to philosophize, although there are always present, to be sure, some philosophical implications. Giving us perhaps his most purely imaginative perceptions, they represent what Emerson might have called the fluidity of nature. For instance, he writes in a fragment describing an ideal poet that

> *He loved to watch and wake*
> *When the wing of the south-wind whipt the lake*
> *And the glassy surface in ripples brake*
> *And fled in pretty frowns away*
> *Like the flitting boreal lights,*
> *Rippling roses in northern nights.*[18]

In respect to Emerson, nevertheless, poetry without philosophy is form without substance. When he is writing of the expression of spirit in nature he reaches one of his highest peaks of imaginative intensity. Philosophy as matter and nature as form combine to produce some of his most thought-provoking imagery. Through it we profoundly realize his conviction that the poet is an imaginative seer, whose imagination is a vision that regards the world as symbolical of the real sense within external form. In "Each and All" we find a visionary identification of subject and object. Most particularly in "Two Rivers" we clearly see the identity of spiritual forces flowing through all life — nature and man. Emerson based his imaginative approach on his belief that to the intellect there could be no diversity, but only unity. For man to be great and the moment profound, the imagination must conceive of the ultimate unity of spiritual life. An Emerson poem thus becomes a concentrated moment in the unfolding experience of spiritual awareness. Above all, as we know, in nature Emerson found his most fertile suggestions of an all-pervading mind. Because of this intellectual attitude, nature, imaginatively conceived, could be only beautiful to him; in it he found his God.

The mind of man, according to Emerson, creates its own world; nature furnishes the raw material that the intellect uses to construct its ideal plan. Emerson, as mythmaker, therefore takes a primarily idealistic or imaginative approach to life or art. As applied to a use of imagery, particularly to imagery based on the close relationship between nature and man, this kind of intellectual attitude is likely to result in imaginative insights through which we find that nature has been made more vital since it is seen as an extension of man's mind, while man himself becomes abstracted to the spiritual essence that the idealist believes he sees in nature.

Emerson's intellectual idealism becomes especially apparent, of course, in his philosophic use of nature. The identity of the spirit of nature with that of man being central in his thought, it is therefore basic in his imagery. The human spirit forms the basis of Emerson's cosmic design, for only through the spiritual perceptions of the imaginative man can nature have any essential meaning.

Emerson's spiritual imagination reaches its height when he uses the image of the flowing of water to represent the universal spirit flowing through man and nature. His imaginative associations with this image in a number of poems give us a significant key to the quality of his poetry. We find the introspection of a subjective poet but also the serenity of a beautiful mind best illustrated perhaps in "Two Rivers." One of Emerson's most fully realized mythic projections, this poem in its music, imagery, and philosophy succeeds in translating his intellectual vision of art.

### TWO RIVERS

*Thy summer voice, Musketaquit,*
*Repeats the music of the rain;*
*But sweeter rivers pulsing flit*
*Through thee, as thou through Concord Plain.*

*Thou in thy narrow banks art pent:*
*The stream I love unbounded goes*
*Through flood and sea and firmament;*
*Through light, through life, it forward flows.*

*I see the inundation sweet,*
*I hear the spending of the stream*
*Through years, through men, through Nature fleet,*
*Through love and thought, through power and dream.*

*Musketaquit, a goblin strong,*
*Of shard and flint makes jewels gay;*
*They lose their grief who hear his song,*
*And where he winds is the day of day.*

*So forth and brighter fares my stream, —*
*Who drink it shall not thirst again;*
*No darkness stains its equal gleam,*
*And ages drop in it like rain.*[19]

Through these images we see the Emersonian vision of a divine energy giving direction to the creative life, both conscious and unconscious; "love and thought," "power and dream" emerge in these creative waves that "no darkness stains." Emerson assures us that the divine spirit ultimately pervades all life; the mind of man on all levels may create a divinely ordered world. Here, imaginatively suggested from the matrix of the creative mind, we discover the core of the myth.

# CHAPTER IV

## *The Shaping Intuition*

### 1

HAVING TRACED THE GENERAL TENDENCY of Emerson's myth-making imagination through his associated idea-images, we may now ask what the effect of these elements may be in their final associations within the organic wholes of poems and what further insight any total poetic structure may give us toward an understanding of Emerson's world-view. Although the preceding analysis of materials has been rather detailed, I believe it serves to show how Emerson's imagination has repeatedly followed characteristic tendencies; central images appear and reappear in significant links throughout his poetry. From this general analysis we have discovered Emerson's favorite images and their typical associations. It seems to me that the grouping of the images according to the dominant regions of life from which they come, although it has involved some repetition of references, has given us a more inclusive view of the tone and temper of Emerson's mind revealed in his poetry than we otherwise could have achieved. These groupings, I believe, do no violence to our comprehension of Emerson's approach at least through his mature years when most of his poetry was written since there are no dramatic cleavages of "periods" in his writings but rather gradual modifications and refinements of his general attitudes, already quite fully established by the time he left the ministry to begin his independent career. But the problem of seeing the ways of his imagination in constructing poetic units remains, for the shaping of the poem is the final triumph of the imagination.

Creation implies some organic principle uniting emotional or intellectual elements of the conscious or unconscious life.[1] Without such unity they lose much significance. In executing a poetic structure the human being follows one way of giving unified significance to his world, which may often seem antithetic to his personal needs and desires. Through the poet's attempt to discover unity between himself and all that is not self, he may at times achieve the illusion of totality, of completeness; the imagination has produced a satisfying synthesis.[2] As the reader participates in this unified projection of the poet, he has a sense of equilibrium or harmony with something larger than the everyday self. This synthesis, following the original stimuli, results from the characteristics of the work of imaginative art.[3] As we saw in the previous investigation of the effects of images in poetry, the final impression of the work of art as a whole is impersonal and does not lead to action. This participation in an impersonal, harmonious experience produces the essence of what we call the effect of "beauty." Even though Emerson's imaginative art is based on a spiritual faith that may not be regarded sympathetically by all present-day psychologists or estheticians, I believe it is not unfair to suggest that his art, which he regarded as organic since it vitally assisted man in bringing himself into harmony with the world, has at least its broad parallels in the psychology of esthetic effect. In this limited sense, if in no other, Emerson was a good psychologist in attempting to lead us through art into experiences of balance and symmetry.

Although critics have often maintained that Emerson "does not conceive of his poems as wholes"[4] and he himself lamented his want of constructive ability, it seems to me that without stretching the argument too far we can still discover principles of ordering the elements of poems into organic unities that disclose something of Emerson's myth-making imagination at work.

The spontaneous, intuitive, almost dreamlike flowing of the depths of the psychological self unites the images of Emerson's imaginative projections. These freely flowing ideas, often stimulated as we have seen in Emerson by some fundamental philosophic concern with the relation of the self to a deeply spiritual entity consisting for him of ultimate "truth," "goodness," or "beauty," appear to the conscious self in the form of concrete images with which they have become fused in the depths of the unconscious self, where the original creation has occurred. From these images the poet may now more consciously mold a total projection from the multiple attitudes of the personal self. As I have said, the resultant imaginative fusion will appear satisfying to the poet because the organic unity has arisen from his deeply felt need for harmony or oneness. Each image-idea will appear to him an added affirmation of the most profound reality. This interpretation, if it is accepted, gives us a pertinent key to the "intellectualized" poetry of Emerson, who had so completely convinced himself of the ultimate benevolent purposes of the creative spirit. The original associated images from this point of view thus tend to carry their own authority. Ideally a minimum of conscious reworking, it would seem, should be involved, for "inspiration" has depended on intuitions, central to life itself; they are those discontinuous, unpredictable waves of revelation from the spirit arising through the unconscious self, analogous, in Emerson's thinking, to the mutations of spirit working in unconscious external nature. The "unconscious" of man is identical, then, to that of nature itself, which is entirely unconscious of the creative spirit working within it. Nature repeats the patterns of life through which it has evolved; but in man consciousness has been achieved, as I have earlier pointed out, and, in this connection, man's conscious self receives and evaluates the deepest communications of the creative spirit or energy. This consciousness may be regarded as a development or refinement of the basic unconscious self or nature and may serve thus to refine or develop the materials given it; but the conscious self alone cannot create in any final sense. The more intuitional a poet is, the more faith he tends to place on his involuntary thought. In a mind like Emerson's, imbued with a belief in a perfect continuity between a spiritual benignity and the personal self, there was every reason to yield to the results of the unconscious creative life and freely express it. This attitude is thus the core not only of Emerson's interpretation of nature and human life but also of the materials and structures of his poetic art.

Generally speaking, it appears that Emerson was usually sure of the tendency of a poem, although from time to time he revised the original drafts with happy results.[5] The more important impression I believe is, however, that of a poet who simply has intellectualized the materials and forms of his art to conform to his most subjective, preconceived notions of what all art must be. Emerson's mythmaking faculty is working in the extreme when we see the entire structures of his poems in which the organization reveals his most complete reliance on intellectual appeals; his poems in image and structure stimulate the mind primarily, not the emotions. As his introspective intellect appears dominant in his use of imagery, so is his subjective view of the world responsible for the resulting poetic structures presenting, as it were, a world in miniature. Since his whole view of man was intellectualized or spiritualized, there can be in my opinion little if any essential difference in Emerson between the ends desired by the conscious or the unconscious parts of the mind; they are rather degrees of development operating in several ways to help the spirit become flesh. As far as we can learn, then, from the evidence of Emerson's characteristic poetic structures, both the unconscious and conscious parts of the mind are attempting on various levels but not antagonistically to disclose the deepest reaches of man's spirit to aid the intangible in becoming tangible. This is, of course, only another way of saying that to Emerson the entire mind of man was an instrument by which a benevolent creator could find fullest expression.

The reader will probably have recalled that no absolute line can be drawn between conscious and unconscious motivations, and also that Emerson did not hastily publish his poems. It seems to me, then, that we must assume that his published poems were the best that he could make them and that their structures are to some degree at least in keeping with his total intent. If we accept Emerson's intuitive thought expressed through images, we also may see that his forms projecting those images are likewise a part of his intuitional approach to life. His form will thus appear to be as characteristic as his style; in fact one depends on the other. If we accept Emerson on his own terms, as I believe we should, much of the superficial criticism that his poems are without structure or music may be avoided. Just as Emerson made free use of his materials in his images, he is independent and experimental in much of his use of rhyme, rhythm, and form. He shows no slavish admiration for either traditional attitudes or structures.[6] In his thought as well as in his artistic methods he is working toward a sense of freedom and individual values through which he is "struggling to maintain, on a nonauthoritarian basis, and in the face of the materialistic drive of his century, the old concept of the dignity of man."[7] In theory and practice the restrained Brahmin is reconciled with the impulsive spirit; his poetry springs from the ecstasy of intellect; his poems are rhapsodies of the soul.

The primary concern of Emerson's imaginative life was to convey his vision of the unity of life; his "The Poet" was first called — significantly enough — "The Discontented Poet." Lines from the second section of "The Poet" may serve to illustrate one kind of poetic unity which Emerson's imagination achieved; they project the process of revelation in the imaginative mind. The images combine to suggest the sense of approaching truth, the imminence of significant expression below the current of the conscious self. The poet yields to a sense of timelessness with joy and hope:

> *The gods talk in the breath of the woods,*
> *They talk in the shaken pine,*
> *And fill the long reach of the old seashore*
> *With dialogue divine;*
> *And the poet who overhears*
> *Some random word they say*
> *Is the fated man of men*
> *Whom the ages must obey:*
> *One who having nectar drank*

*Into blissful orgies sank;*
*He takes no mark of night or day,*
*He cannot go, he cannot stay,*
*He would, yet would not, counsel keep,*
*But, like a walker in his sleep*
*With staring eye that seeth none,*
*Ridiculously up and down*
*Seeks how he may fitly tell*
*The heart-o'erlading miracle.*

*Not yet, not yet,*
*Impatient friend, —*
*A little while attend;*
*Not yet I sing: but I must wait,*
*My hand upon the silent string,*
*Fully until the end.*
*I see the coming light,*
*I see the scattered gleams,*
*Aloft, beneath, on left and right*
*The stars' own ether beams;*
*These are but seeds of days,*
*Not yet a steadfast morn,*
*An intermittent blaze,*
*An embryo god unborn.*
*How all things sparkle,*
*The dust is alive,*
*To the birth they arrive:*
*I snuff the breath of my morning afar,*
*I see the pale lustres condense to a star:*
*The fading colors fix,*
*The vanishing are seen,*
*And the world that shall be*
*Twins the world that has been.*
*I know the appointed hour,*
*I greet my office well,*

*Never faster, never slower*
*Revolves the fatal wheel!*
*The Fairest enchants me,*
*The Mighty commands me,*
*Saying, 'Stand in thy place;*
*Up and eastward turn thy face;*
*As mountains for the morning wait,*
*Coming early, coming late,*
*So thou attend the enriching Fate*
*Which none can stay, and none accelerate.'*
*I am neither faint nor weary,*
*Fill thy will, O faultless heart!*
*Here from youth to age I tarry, —*
*Count it flight of bird or dart.*
*My heart at the heart of things*
*Heeds no longer lapse of time,*
*Rushing ages moult their wings,*
*Bathing in thy day sublime.*
*The sun set, but set not his hope: —*
*Stars rose, his faith was earlier up:*
*Fixed on the enormous galaxy,*
*Deeper and older seemed his eye,*
*And matched his sufferance sublime*
*The taciturnity of Time.*[8]

The reader will have noted in these lines how, for instance, the images of rebirth and dawn are intermingled to suggest the awakening of the imaginative, spiritual life. Yet with all the intellectual rapture that is aroused, the poet remains receptive to the larger voice that will speak in its time. He projects himself as being in a kind of intoxication or sleep-walking, blissful because he senses the "coming light." A passage from "Each and All" may illustrate this favorite method of Emerson to suggest his arriving at inspirational insight. His attention having been concentrated on the apparent tricks that aspects of nature, formerly thought beautiful, may play on one, he is about to turn his back on beauty as a false guide, but, he says:

> As I spoke, beneath my feet
> The ground-pine curled its pretty wreath,
> Running over the club-moss burrs;
> I inhaled the violet's breath;
> Around me stood the oaks and firs;
> Pine-cones and acorns lay on the ground;
> Over me soared the eternal sky,
> Full of light and of deity;
> Again I saw, again I heard,
> The rolling river, the morning bird; —
> Beauty through my senses stole;
> I yielded myself to the perfect whole.[9]

Here the varied impressions of nature's unity bring him back to a realization of a principle of life; beauty is not accidental, but intrinsic. The poem develops from a sense of the diversity and separateness of nature to the conviction of nature's organic whole. The high peak of the concluding lines comes as an intellectual ecstasy after the low mood of disunity and isolation. And the nature images in this intense moment do not appear as merely pleasant decoration; they arrive with authority to announce their deepest truth of unified beauty that alone satisfies the philosophic mind. We seem to participate directly in this revelation as the awareness of a spiritual unity becomes manifest to the poet.

In addition to recording steps in the process of revelation, Emerson also shows us parallel recapturings of revelation itself. To put it more precisely, the impression is rather, it seems to me, that the excited and freely working

imagination repeatedly shoots toward the target of fulfill-
ment, or the impulsive waves of the intellectual life beat
upon the shores of consciousness. Seen in this light "Brahma"
is one of Emerson's most warmly ecstatic poems; the intellect is fired with its vision of the world-soul. The imagination, as it were, fairly strains at its own leash to communicate in a rapid succession of images the spiritual energy that
impels it:

> *If the red slayer think he slays,*
>   *Or if the slain think he is slain,*
> *They know not well the subtle ways*
>   *I keep, and pass, and turn again.*
>
> *Far or forgot to me is near;*
>   *Shadow and sunlight are the same;*
> *The vanished gods to me appear;*
>   *And one to me are shame and fame.*
>
> *They reckon ill who leave me out;*
>   *When me they fly, I am the wings;*
> *I am the doubter and the doubt,*
>   *And I the hymn the Brahmin sings.*
>
> *The strong gods pine for my abode,*
>   *And pine in vain the sacred Seven;*
> *But thou, meek lover of the good!*
>   *Find me, and turn thy back on heaven.*[10]

Although this is one of Emerson's most familiar poems, I
have quoted it entirely here because I wanted the reader
to recapture at this point the psychological experience that
I believe is central in understanding Emerson. The unity of
such a poem is more than the parallel phrasings giving a
sense of balance. Its essential unity arises from the very
quality of the imaginative impulses that throb through the

beats of the lines. The urgency of the need to communicate makes the poem a vital experience as it arises from a deeply held conviction of the poet. The images almost seem to shoot out from a common center, something like the sparks from a skyrocket. Here is no slow development or argumentative process. This is light itself! If the closing lines of "Each and All" may be taken as the record of organic beauty, "Brahma" is a revelation, even more enraptured, of an inherent truth. The poetic form derives essentially from certain methods of the imagination itself, and once again the images are not peripheral but at the heart of the revelation, each striking, as it were, at the center of concern, and they further illustrate how nature and man are inseparably associated in Emerson's imagination as it alternately leaps from an image taken from nature to one from human life to express the unfaltering trust in more than "heaven."

Much of the same outburst of images building to a powerful cumulative effect occurs in "The Humble-Bee," which might be taken to illustrate Emerson's projection of the thrilling goodness he could find in nature. The images fairly vibrate with enthusiasm when Emerson in sheer happiness has discovered:

> *Insect lover of the sun,*
> *Joy of thy dominion!*
> *Sailor of the atmosphere;*
> *Swimmer through the waves of air;*
> *Voyager of light and noon;*
> *Epicurean of June.*[11]

Perhaps most completely in "Mithridates" we experience the full extreme of the kind of intellectual rapture characteristic of Emerson. Superficially seen, this poem may ap-

pear to suggest only the most eccentric yielding to excitement; more sympathetically seen, from the point of view
of Emerson's delight in the experimental life as the only
way of discovering one's own truths, it is a plea for genuine
rather than imitative experience. Here is the principle of
thorough rebellion against conformity. Emerson's mythmaking imagination can present not only the self-contained
universal spirit speaking as Brahma or the joyful adventurer
of the humble-bee but also the symbolically wise man who,
filled with life, can find some value in all kinds of experience.
The poem is understandable, then, in terms of Emerson's
intellectualized mythmaking faculty. There is probably no
need to quote the entire poem here, but I should like to call
the reader's attention at least to typical passages in which
again the freely playing images, here among the most startling Emerson ever produced, serve their purpose, I believe,
in arousing the reader out of lethargy and complacency:

> Give me agates for my meat;
> Give me cantharids to eat;
> . . . . . . . . . . . . . . . . . . . . . .
> Ivy for my fillet band;
> Blinding dog-wood in my hand;
> Hemlock for my sherbet cull me,
> And the prussic juice to lull me;
> Swing me in the upas boughs,
> Vampyre-fanned, when I carouse.[12]

Contrasting with this use of imagery we note, however, that
in "Guy," an equally mythmaking poem, Emerson may use
a more restrained image when suggesting the balanced human spirit who has achieved a sense of power and peace:

> Guy possessed the talisman
> That all things from him began;

*And as, of old, Polycrates*
*Chained the sunshine and the breeze,*
*So did Guy betimes discover*
*Fortune was his guard and lover.*[13]

We have seen how the use of images builds the effect in constructing either the process of revelation or the overwhelming conviction of a vital experience in which Emerson is not making comments about the experience but attempting to give the reader as accurately as he can the essence of the experience itself. In this regard we may also note how the opening strength of such a work as "Days," a poem that from Emerson's own testimony seemed almost to write itself, increases in intensity from "Daughters of Time, the hypocritic Days" to the culminating thrust in "I, too late,/Under her solemn fillet saw the scorn."[14] Here is a genuine mythmaker at work as he leads us through increasingly dynamic images to live the experience.

On the other hand, Emerson's imagination projects an equally vital interpretation of the world by weaving harmonious images around an implied center of reference; through the interplay of images an implied whole is suggested. This method is the reverse of that used in "Brahma," with its urge to convince by the repeated thrusts from a common center, the brilliance of each image almost blinding us to the next. In this contrasting method we find an interweaving of blended images that stimulate by the very richness of their associations. I can find no better example of this method than in "The Snow-Storm." In the closing nineteen lines particularly, Emerson's imagination has conveyed through images much of the creative life of art. Here the imagination does not have to fire or urge; it completely controls its medium; it has completely realized itself. We appear to be at the heart of the mystery. The esthetic effect results from the perfect unity of material and structure leaving us with a sense of equilibrium in the resolution of the whole; no matter how untamed and impulsive the creative imagination may seem to be, it seeks to find the satisfaction of release in organic unity:

> Come see the north wind's masonry.
> Out of an unseen quarry evermore
> Furnished with tile, the fierce artificer
> Curves his white bastions with projected roof
> Round every windward stake, or tree, or door.
> Speeding, the myriad-handed, his wild work
> So fanciful, so savage, nought cares he
> For number or proportion. Mockingly,
> On coop or kennel he hangs Parian wreaths;
> A swan-like form invests the hidden thorn;
> Fills up the farmer's lane from wall to wall,
> Maugre the farmer's sighs; and at the gate
> A tapering turret overtops the work.
> And when his hours are numbered, and the world
> Is all his own, retiring, as he were not,
> Leaves, when the sun appears, astonished Art
> To mimic in slow structures, stone by stone,
> Built in an age, the mad wind's night-work,
> The frolic architecture of the snow.[15]

While this poem, like "Two Rivers," illustrates a satisfying adjustment between means and ends, "Bacchus" and "Merlin" take us into a realm where Emerson's imagination seems to challenge art itself to further adventure as his imagination prophesies things yet to come. There is abundant evidence in such poems as "Brahma," with its regular quatrains of alternate rhymes and iambic tetrameter rhythm, or "Two Rivers," with its perfect flow of iambic tetrameter and musical harmony of alternate rhymes, that Emerson could shape his imaginative visions in conventional wholes. While this regularity creates the illusion of the flow of the stream of spirit in "Two Rivers" and causes the steady pulses of the images in "Brahma," Emerson's imagination does not seem content with what from the evidence of "Bacchus" and "Merlin" must almost have seemed a compromise.

That Emerson's imagination found expression throughout his poetry in a free, unconventional rhythmical pulsation, combined with striking images and startling rhymes, poems like "Each and All" (1839), "The Problem" (1841), "Hamatreya" (1847), and "Terminus" (1867) give evidence.[16] The essential point to be noted, however, is that in a poem like "Merlin" or "Bacchus" the power of image after image is often reinforced by capturing the reader's attention in an unexpected rhythm, coupled with dramatic emphasis on sound combinations and contrasts in the rhyme; the experimental shaping imagination of Emerson is triumphant.[17] Here is indeed poetry "so passionate and alive that like the spirit of a plant or an animal it has an architecture of its own, and adorns nature with a new thing."[18] The reader may select instances of this sort of organic effectiveness that seem most impressive to him; but let us note, for example, some of the effects produced by image, rhyme, and rhythm working as a sort of intuitive whole through which "idea" in image is fully communicated by pulsation and sound in the following lines from "Merlin":

> *He shall not seek to weave,*
> *In weak, unhappy times,*

*Efficacious rhymes;*
*Wait his returning strength.*
*Bird that from the nadir's floor*
*To the zenith's top can soar, —*
*The soaring orbit of the muse exceeds that*
    *journey's length.*
*Nor profane affect to hit*
*Or compass that, by meddling wit,*
*Which only the propitious mind*
*Publishes when 't is inclined.*
*There are open hours*
*When the God's will sallies free,*
*And the dull idiot might see*
*The flowing fortunes of a thousand years; —*
*Sudden, at unawares,*
*Self-moved, fly-to the doors,*
*Nor sword of angels could reveal*
*What they conceal.*[19]

First there is, it seems to me, a powerful irony suggested in the second and third lines of this passage by the change in rhythm from the faster rising beat of "In weak, unhappy times" to the slower, heavier beat of "Efficacious rhymes." The mind is brought to a halt almost as if by a reprimand. Then note the sudden expansion into the strongly beating sweep of "The soaring orbit of the muse exceeds that journey's length." The contrast is now even more complete by being associated in the memory with the bite of "Efficacious rhymes." The impression is further sharpened by the pointed thrusts of the heavily accented "hit" being rhymed with "meddling wit," the superficial "conscious" mind that Emerson here disparages. But follow especially the imaginative interplay of effects in the closing lines, starting with "There are open hours," when Emerson seems to break free from mere irony or reprimand to triumphant conviction. The lines increase their subtle surge up to "The flowing fortunes of a thousand years; —" then comes the splendid shock of the rhyme, not only as the image changes but also as the very movement of thought simultaneously alters its pace. We are startled to attention by the juxtaposing of the sounds of "years" with "unawares"; we *are* taken unawares! The doors of inspiration fly shut of themselves; we become doubly convinced that even the "sword of angels" cannot open them when the lines close on the positive rhyme: "reveal" — "conceal." Here Emerson's mythmaking imagination has nearly exceeded itself in prophesying what the poetic imagination playing "free, peremptory, clear" may produce.[20]

2

Since Emerson's lyrics, concerned with aspects of life larger than the biographical self, achieve effects of organic structure through his artistic intuitions emphasizing image through rhythm and rhyme, what can we finally say about the fundamental motivations of Emerson's imaginative art? In tracing some of the possible interpretations of Emerson's view of the workings of the imagination in the opening sections of this study, we found that the Emersonian explanation of life's creative forces is incomplete without some reference to a "deeper" power on which the human psyche depends. To some readers who are discontented with any sort of *a priori* suppositions of the abilities of the mind, this belief, inescapable in any complete interpretation of Emerson's own theory, may seem the most complete myth

Emerson ever created. As the reader long since will have seen, the "imagination" in Emerson's thinking provides a means of revealing "spiritual" truths. Although Emerson's poetry contains, as I have tried to show, many esthetic appeals in style and structure, it is certain that Emerson, who defined a poem as a "metre-making argument," would never have been satisfied with poetic effects divorced from poetic purposes. Image, rhythm, rhyme are present in a poem, Emerson would believe, because they are inseparable elements of the total imaginative communication, just as the tones and accents of one's speaking voice, for instance, are parts of the total effect of what he is saying. The central purpose of the workings of the imagination to Emerson, I believe, was to communicate in humanly understandable terms something of the ultimate vitality and unity of life's deepest potentialities, which Emerson believed were working toward achieving more of the "good" and "beautiful" in human life. He saw that external nature had fulfilled its purpose in revealing spirit in the "unconscious"; the present task for man's mind was to continue this effort through the harmoniously combined effort of the total unconscious and conscious human self. Particularly in respect to poetry, the poetic creator's happy task was to express through deepest intuitive imagination the spirit of life as it presented itself to him. As I see it, then, Emerson's break from the ministry was not motivated by a desire for less but for more spiritual experience. As every reader of Emerson knows, he felt that conventional religion had helped to enervate the finest spiritual achievements of life; modern man, in his belief, could satisfactorily find real spiritual significance only within himself. Emerson's purpose was to help man discover his own dignity.[21]

It may be just at this point where the twentieth-century reader can most fully appreciate Emerson's problem as an imaginative artist. In his day Emerson felt the need for a renewal of the arts, as many forward-looking critics do today.[22] Every student of American life knows that Emerson became a leader of what is now often called a "Renaissance" period in American culture because he successfully contributed toward shifting early emphases of American intellectual life from the debasement of inherently evil man under an absolutely sovereign God in Puritanism and the limitation of man's spirit under a narrow rationalism in scientific Unitarianism. In Emerson's thinking about literary art, however, the aspect needing principal emphasis perhaps even more today than in Emerson's time is the problem of the imaginative uses of mind. While this study has shown the reliance of the imaginative mind on ultimate spiritual sources in Emerson's interpretation, since he recognizes a "divine" power immanent in man's spirit, this idealistic support should not blind one to the implications of this basic tendency of Emerson's thinking to identify the "human" with the "divine" in any ideal instance. When Emerson maintains that "the Divine, or, as some will say, the truly Human, hovers, now seen, now unseen, before us,"[23] he is more than repeating a type of "mystical" reliance on superhuman power. Indeed when Emerson speaks of the ways in which a "mystic" uses language he characteristically feels dissatisfied with the result, not only perhaps because of the well-recognized difficulty — or impossibility — of the traditional mystic's attempt to communicate an experience beyond expression but also because whenever the mystic does try to communicate through literature he is likely to end by establishing a rigid formula of symbols to guide human experience, like those found in Swedenborg, whom Emerson selected as his representative "mystic," but significantly rejected as one without a genuinely creative, imaginative mind. It bears repeating that Emerson always remained discontent with the tendency of a "mystic" to harness and shackle language to a spiritual formalism. The free flowing of imaginative spirit through all forms of life represents the basic difference between Emerson's concept of the truly imaginative production and the formalistic pattern of a mystic's message. To Emerson, I believe, mystical writing, like Swedenborg's, could not be considered as "imaginative literature" in any final sense.

In addition, while one — if he is so minded — may include Emerson himself in the general company of "mystics," who are, after all, of many varieties,[24] because of his admitting of a kind of flowing into the creative mind of an inspiration having great power beyond conscious control, we must also remember Emerson's further tendency to identify this power, sometimes called "God," as a subjective reality in those times when man as poet cheers mankind: "One more royal trait properly belongs to the poet. I mean his cheerfulness, without which no man can be a poet, — for beauty is his aim."[25] In the happy moment of poetic creation, when the poet speaks from character and health, he has become psychologically a balanced man in whom intellect ("conscious" mind) and soul (spirit arising through "unconscious" mind) are working harmoniously.[26] In his admiration of Wordsworth, who also wrote best in moments of "joy," Emerson remarks that "the great praise of Wordsworth, [is] that more than any other contemporary bard he is pervaded with a reverence of somewhat higher than (conscious) thought."[27] Although Emerson by no means limits the soul speaking through a poet merely to the poet's private psychological self, but recognizes the universal quality of spirit,[28] the emphasis, it seems to me, in literary production lies in Emerson's insistence that the mature, balanced creative person tends to feel an identity between the universal creative spirit and his own. On the other hand, Deity becomes objectified in man's low moods when man lacks character and health, the essentials to Emerson for a genuinely creative life worthy of serious notice. "Ignorance and passion alloy and degrade. In proportion to a man's want of goodness, it [Spirit] seems to him another and not himself; that is to say, the Deity becomes more objective, until finally flat idolatry prevails."[29] While Emerson is speaking in this context of the constant problem of degrading any spiritual insight in a material artifact, he is equally concerned with the state of man who may not only worship "idols" of religion and art but may also continue to create art products unworthy of man's highest possibilities. Ideally, of course, any art form may never completely fulfill its creator's ultimate vision of beauty, and the artist may be moved to silence at the failure of his efforts. Yet, if art is to be created at all, art worthy of Emerson's ideal must spring from more than immature, egocentric bids for attention.

Emerson's attitude toward dreams underlines this kind of distinction between the mature and the immature artist in his thinking. In dreams Emerson believed the private, egocentric side of man reveals itself. Literature based only on dream material seemed to him a way of glorifying the individual self indulging its sick ideas and weak motives. To Emerson the dream arises from darkness; he preferred the daylight. The egocentric dream obscures the universal vision. Private "demons" appear in one's dreams, but Emerson wonders how they can serve to benefit mankind: "The demonologic is only a fine name for egotism; an exaggeration namely of the individual, whom it is Nature's settled purpose to postpone. 'There is one world common to all who are awake, but each sleeper betakes himself to one of his own.' [Heraclitus.] Dreams retain the infirmities of our character. The good genius may be there or not, our evil genius is sure to stay. The Ego partial makes the dream; the Ego total the interpretation. Life is also a dream on the same terms."[30] Emerson thus reinforces his belief that there are deeper realities in life than those superficially touched by the individual dream, which tends to see life as usually tragic or evil. The ultimate depths, to Emerson, are intrinsically good; the divine is revealed when the total being is healthy and right, or of best character.[31]

Although the observing of dream material may be a step toward realizing other sides of the self and thus help toward a stage of objectivity for esthetic experience,[32] since man, by considering his dreams, can begin to appreciate himself as both creator and spectator, the dream itself is an illusive step toward final reality for Emerson. Indeed, psychologically speaking, Emerson seems to feel that the best service of the dream experience results from the impression of regions of life different from the everyday conscious self. In the "otherness" of the dream, despite the final undesirability of its egocentric content, there arises at least a hint of powers greater than the ordinary self-conscious intellect. The dream begins to lead the mind toward more imaginative perspectives and ideal relationships, but Emerson at last distrusted dreams since a "dislocation seems to be the foremost trait of dreams. A painful imperfection almost always attends them. The fairest forms, the most noble and excellent persons, are deformed by some pitiful and insane circumstance."[33] The flowing of intuitive "inspirations" from the soul are only apparently but not actually the same as one's private dream, a spectre of personal inadequacy in Emerson's judgment. The vision of the ideal poetic seer, on the contrary, guides from individual darkness to universal light. It is only in this sense of spiritual illumination that Emerson's "poet" can be called momentarily a "dreamer" who, as Emerson pictures him in the poem on "The Poet," awaits in his "sleep-walking" the intuitions that are "divine" because they are filled with hope and joy. Life, in this wider sense, appears to be a dream in which man sleeps until the divine awakes him.

When aroused to this ultimate reality, either through the experience of poetic creation itself or through the stimulation of poetic art, Emerson felt a spiritual exaltation, for he had pierced beneath appearances to final truth.[34] As this study has tried to show, the main psychological appeal in Emerson's poetry derives from the effective use of imagery directing one's attention to the philosophic concepts typical of Emerson. The images, as mental events, change, but the philosophic vision remains. In his most idealistic attitude toward the materials of poetic art, Emerson reminds us of the position Shelley took when he wrote in "Adonais": "The One remains, the many change and pass; . . ./Life, like a dome of many-colored glass,/Stains the white radiance of Eternity."[35] Yet, within the limits of poetic communication, the word may often seem one with the thought as the imaginative mind finds expression through the methods of art. Although to Emerson the fluidity of the philosophic imagination remains paramount, and the thought, in his opinion, should ideally remain free of its momentary material image, in the complete body of his poems the images.

in a sense, fix for the reader one approach toward discovering the unified mind from which they came. As a matter of fact, in Emerson's own esthetic approach to literature he admits first the stimulation of sense impressions to be followed by the interpretation of the receptive mind as the soul becomes aroused.[36]

Poetry, as a metaphor of life, may thus be used by the imaginative mind as one way of perceiving values that otherwise may continue hidden. In his own day, for instance, Emerson was disillusioned about fundamental decencies by the Mexican and Civil wars with their tragic aftermaths. Yet he lived in the hope that men would find ways toward a better life, as he had announced in the leading article of *The Dial* for October, 1840:

What, then, shall hinder the Genius of the time from speaking its thought? It cannot be silent, if it would. It will write in a higher spirit and a wider knowledge and with a grander practical aim than ever yet guided the pen of poet. It will write the annals of a changed world, and record the descent of principles into practice, of love into Government, of love into Trade. It will describe the new heroic life of man, the now unbelieved possibility of simple living and of clean and noble relations with men. Religion will bind again these that were sometime frivolous, customary, enemies, skeptics, self-seekers, into a joyful reverence for the circumambient Whole, and that which was ecstasy shall become daily bread.[37]

As I have tried to show, I believe Emerson's approach was based on his confidence in the free, intuitive intellect. Although to some readers Emerson's attitude may appear impossibly visionary, the principle in earlier criticism of Emerson that has not been sufficiently emphasized, if it has not been altogether ignored, is that Emerson can be approached and to a considerable degree understood from a broadly psychological standpoint. In other words, the present-day reader, although he has seen how Emerson hardly coincides completely with any single trend of contemporary psychology or psychoanalysis, may still feel at home in much of Emerson's thought because his world-view was anchored in his belief in the significance and validity of the human mind in its fullest sense.

While to some readers this emphasis may seem to rob Emerson of much authority by removing conventional religious associations from him, this is precisely what he chose to do himself and, it seems to me, exactly why he retains much interest for present readers. Probably twentieth-century man can not fully rest in Emerson's world, but in it he finds a good deal that generally anticipates some of the more challenging, experimental tendencies of present thought.[38] I believe, then, that Emerson is less the religious "mystic" than is usually supposed offhand and more the "psychological" interpreter, although his psychology may indeed appear highly imaginary to many readers today. About this there need be no argument; in his total view of the mind as a reservoir of greatest idealism discovered and revealed by the intuitive intellect he may have created his greatest myth. Yet I am sure that no one, least of all a careful, conscientious psychologist, is prepared to affirm or deny the ultimate basis of Emerson's idealism, the vital source of his creative life. As Jung candidly said in *Modern Man in Search of a Soul*:

The psychologist, to be sure, may never abandon his claim to investigate and establish causal relations in complicated psychic events. To do so would be to deny psychology the right to exist. Yet he can never make good this claim in the fullest sense, because the creative aspect of life which finds its clearest expression in art baffles all attempts at rational formulation. Any reaction to stimulus may be causally explained; but the creative act, which is the absolute antithesis of mere reaction, will for ever elude the human understanding. It can only be described in its manifestations; it can be obscurely sensed, but never wholly grasped.[39]

If the reaches of the creative imagination are likely to remain obscure, so may the sources of the varieties of religious experience, which William James described at length. At all events, to Emerson the total spirit of man presented a constant source of human values. Everything must have value to man, for to Emerson heaven was indeed here and now. Seen in this light, Emerson's "transcendentalism" illustrates a belief in the intuitively mental and spiritually powerful potentialities of man who transcends his ordinary human experience by transforming it through imagination. Emerson's creative vision resolved ethics with esthetics. "The religions of the world," he said, "are the ejaculations of a few imaginative men."[40] The body of Emerson's poetry is a metaphor of the essential possibilities for virtue and beauty in the mind and spirit of man as Emerson saw him.[41] Triumphantly asserting man's organic unity with his world, Emerson's poetry becomes a magnificent projection of the mythmaking imagination creating through art a faith, Emerson believed, for every man, who within the darkness may yet see a living light.

# Notes

## CHAPTER I

### The Personal Myth

1. *Seven Types of Ambiguity: A Study of Its Effects in English Verse* (London: Chatto & Windus, 1930), p. 322.

2. Cf. Thomas E. Hulme, "Bergson's Theory of Art," *Speculations: Essays on Humanism and the Philosophy of Art* (London: Kegan Paul, Trench, Trubner & Co.; New York: Harcourt, Brace & Co., 1936), pp. 143–169.

3. "Art and Criticism" in *The Complete Works of Ralph Waldo Emerson*, ed. Edward W. Emerson, Centenary Edition (Boston: Houghton Mifflin Co., 1903–1904), XII, 305. (Hereafter cited as *Works*.) While Emerson favors modern reinterpretation as fundamental to the observer in esthetic experience, he holds that all real masterpieces contain the power to stir the observer to a sense of their timeless, universal qualities. See Vivian C. Hopkins, *Spires of Form: A Study of Emerson's Aesthetic Theory* (Cambridge: Harvard University Press, 1951), pp. 152–154.

4. Sigmund Freud, *Collected Papers* (London: The Hogarth Press, Ltd., 1925), IV, 174.

5. *The Poetical Works of Wordsworth*, ed. Thomas Hutchinson (New York: Oxford University Press, 1904), p. 578.

6. *Movement and Mental Imagery* (Boston: Houghton Mifflin Co., 1916), p. 219.

7. *Creative Mind* (New York: D. Appleton & Co.; Cambridge: University Press, 1931), p. 10.

8. (New York: Harcourt, Brace & Co., 1925), pp. 191–192.

9. *The Poetic Image* (New York: Oxford University Press, 1947), p. 17.

10. (New York: Simon & Schuster, Inc., 1940), p. 235.

11. See Henri Bergson, *Laughter* (New York: The Macmillan Co., 1921), p. 151.

12. "General Preface to the Novels and Poems," in *Tess of the D'Urbervilles* (New York, London: Harper & Bros., 1935), p. xii.

13. Cf. remarks on studying Shakespeare's imagery in Lillian H. Hornstein, "Analysis of Imagery: A Critique of Literary Method," *PMLA*, LVII, No. 3 (Sept., 1942), 638–653. However, Donald A. Stauffer shows in his "Postscript" to *Shakespeare's World of Images: The Development of His Moral Ideas* (New York: W. W. Norton & Co., 1949) to what extent a discriminating critic can reasonably evaluate a dramatist's use of materials.

14. *Essay on the Creative Imagination* (Chicago: The Open Court Publishing Co.; London: Kegan Paul, Trench, Trubner & Co., 1906), pp. 43–44.

15. See *ibid.*, pp. 27 ff.

16. *The Journals of Ralph Waldo Emerson*, eds. Edward W. Emerson and Waldo E. Forbes (Boston: Houghton Mifflin Co., 1909–1914), VIII, 9.

17. See Frederick C. Prescott, *The Poetic Mind* (New York: The Macmillan Co., 1922), pp. 171 ff.

18. See Alfred N. Whitehead, *Symbolism, Its Meaning and Effect* (New York: The Macmillan Co., 1927), esp., pp. 28–29, 57–59.

19. Washburn, pp. 183–184.

20. *Theory and Art of Mysticism* (London, New York: Longmans, Green & Co., Inc., 1937), p. 81.

21. See Ribot, pp. 36–37.

22. See Prescott, pp. 156–157.

23. *Works*, XII, 103. Cf. lines on memory as the source of imagination in "Bacchus," *Works*, IX, 126–127.

24. See Prescott, p. 218.

25. See *ibid.*, pp. 278 ff.

26. Emerson distinguished between the mind's "percipiency," from which it obtains primary sense impressions, and "perception," which gives rise to a general intellectual or spiritual concept from individual impressions. Perception depends on a degree of detachment that can see larger relationships. (See "Natural History of Intellect," *Works*, XII, 39–41.) Such detachment is essential, Emerson believed, to art. "The virtue of art lies in detachment, in sequestering one object from the embarrassing variety." ("Art," *ibid.*, II, 354.) This detached perception results from the working of what Emerson called the Will, the creative energy, which is unpredictable, for, as Emerson maintained, "Will is always miraculous, being the presence of God to men.... Heaven is the exercise of the faculties, the added sense of power." (*Ibid.*, XII, 46.) This deeper creative will on which the best achievement of the individual depends is in contrast to the interfering, superficial will of the private ego of the self-conscious artist. (See "Poetry and Imagination," *ibid.*, VIII, 69.)

27. Hutchinson (ed.), p. 187.

28. See Frederick C. Prescott, *Poetry and Myth* (New York: The Macmillan Co., 1927), p. 114.

29. *Elizabethan and Metaphysical Imagery: Renaissance Poetic and Twentieth-Century Critics* (Chicago: University of Chicago Press, 1947). See esp. "The Problem and What It Involves," pp. 3–26.

30. *The Works of John Ruskin*, eds. E. T. Cook and Alexander Wedderburn (New York: Longmans, Green & Co., Inc., 1904), V, 209.

31. "The Poet," *Works*, III, 33.

## CHAPTER II

### The Springs of Imagination

1. *The Transcendentalists: An Anthology*, ed. Perry Miller (Cambridge: Harvard University Press, 1950), p. 55.

2. *Works*, I, 32.

3. Miller (ed.), p. 56.

4. *The Religious Philosophy of Plotinus and Some Modern Philosophies of Religion* (London: The Lindsey Press [1914?]), pp. 38–39.

5. *Ibid.*, p. 35.

6. *T. S. Eliot: The Design of His Poetry* (New York: Charles Scribner's Sons, 1949). See esp. Chap. I, "The Mythical Vision," pp. 1–15.

7. *The Ego and the Id* (London: The Hogarth Press, 1927), p. 79.

8. *Ibid.*, pp. 29–30.

9. *Ibid.*, p. 47.

10. *Freud: His Dream and Sex Theories* (New York: Pocket Books, Inc., 1948; Greenburg: Publisher, 1932), p. 278.

11. *Ibid.*, p. 184n.

12. *Ibid.*, p. 167. For other critics of Freud the reader may consult Karen Horney, *New Ways in Psychoanalysis* (New York: W. W. Norton & Co., 1939) and Erich Fromm, *Man for Himself* (New York: Rinehart & Co., 1947).

13. See Gregory Zilboorg, *Mind, Medicine, and Man* (New York: Harcourt, Brace & Co., 1943), p. 330.

14. *Ibid.*, p. 324.

15. *Ibid.*, pp. 320–322.

16. *The Philosophic Basis of Mysticism* (Edinburgh: T. & T. Clark, 1937), p. 294.

17. Pp. 36–37.

18. *Works*, III, 27.

19. "Shakespeare," in Miller (ed.), pp. 346–353.

20. *Works*, I, 31.

21. "Merlin," *Works*, IX, 121.

22. "The Poet and the Poetic Gift," *Works*, IX, 333. Cf. "Nature I": "Casualty and Surprise/Are the apples of her eyes." *Ibid.*, 225.

23. *The Complete Poetical Works of William Wordsworth*, ed. Andrew J. George (Boston: Houghton Mifflin Co., 1904), ll. 815–824, p. 231.

24. See Norman Foerster, "Emerson on the Organic Principle in Art," *PMLA*, XLI, No. 1 (March, 1926), 193–208.

25. *Works*, I, 96–97.

26. (New Haven: Yale University Press, 1938), pp. 47–49.

27. *Psychology of the Unconscious* (New York: Moffat, Yard & Co. [now Dodd, Mead & Co.], 1916), p. 193.

28. See Jung, *Collected Papers on Analytical Psychology* (New

York: Moffat, Yard & Co. [now Dodd, Mead & Co.], 1917), p. 438.
29. P. 87.
30. *Essay on the Creative Imagination*, p. 51.
31. *Aesthetic Motive* (New York: The Macmillan Co., 1939), pp. 57–58.
32. *Works*, IX, 6.
33. Cf. Prescott, *The Poetic Mind*, p. 90.
34. *Ibid.*, pp. 73–74.
35. *Works*, II, 50.
36. *Ibid.*, I, 27.
37. *Ibid.*, III, 8.
38. *Ibid.*, 293.
39. See "Swedenborg," *Works*, IV, 93 ff.
40. (London: Sampson Low, Marston, Searle, and Rivington, 1889), p. 249.
41. *Works*, III, 10.
42. *Ibid.*, 21.
43. See Jastrow, pp. 166 ff.
44. Cf. Hornstein, *loc. cit.*, p. 641.
45. See Carl F. Strauch, "The Date of Emerson's *Terminus*," *PMLA*, LXV, No. 4 (June, 1950), 360–370. Cf. the valuable comments on revising manuscripts of poems in the essays by Rudolph Arnheim, W. H. Auden, Karl Shapiro, and Donald A. Stauffer in *Poets at Work: Essays Based on the Modern Poetry Collection at the Lockwood Memorial Library, University of Buffalo* (New York: Harcourt, Brace & Co., 1948). See esp. pp. 90–94, 143–147.
46. See note in *Works*, IX, 479. From his examination of Emerson's manuscripts of "Days," Strauch believes it likely that this poem may have been inspired by Emerson's rereading of "May-Day," which is juxtaposed in the manuscripts. The personification as well as the images of dancing and disguise are psychologically linked in both poems. We here have further evidence of the associative faculties of Emerson's mind. "Days" is a more satisfying projection of Emerson's attitude than "May-Day" because, as Strauch says, "At one moment of highly concentrated inspiration, the chaotic fragment yielded the perfect little cosmos." Carl F. Strauch, "The Manuscript Relationships of Emerson's 'Days,'" *Philological Quarterly*, XXIX, No. 2 (April, 1950), 207.
47. *Works*, IX, 479.
48. For the explanation of the scene and the passage from the journal, see *Works*, IX, 484.
49. See Prescott, *The Poetic Mind*, p. 239.
50. *Works*, IX, 479.
51. See Ribot, pp. 63–64.
52. See Jung, *Psychology of the Unconscious*, p. 156, and Freud, *The Ego and the Id*, pp. 21–22.

53. *Works*, III, 18.

54. *Ibid.*, 26.

55. Susanne K. Langer, *Philosophy in a New Key: A Study in the Symbolism of Reason, Rite, and Art* (Cambridge: Harvard University Press, 1942), p. 145.

56. See Samuel Alexander, *Beauty and Other Forms of Value* (London: Macmillan & Co., 1933), p. 125.

57. See Hulme, *Speculations*, pp. 161–163.

58. See Hanns Sachs, *The Creative Unconscious: Studies in the Psychoanalysis of Art* (Cambridge, Mass.: Sci-Art Publishers, 1942), pp. 58–60.

59. "Worship," *Works*, VI, 219.

60. "Freud and Literature," in *Criticism: The Foundations of Modern Literary Judgment*, eds. Mark Schorer, Josephine Miles, and Gordon McKenzie. (New York: Harcourt, Brace & Co., 1948), p. 173. Cf. the interesting revision of this statement in Trilling's collection *The Liberal Imagination* (New York: The Viking Press, 1950), p. 36.

61. Frederick W. Conner, *Cosmic Optimism: A Study of the Interpretation of Evolution by American Poets from Emerson to Robinson* (Gainesville: University of Florida Press, 1949), p. 64.

62. See Joseph W. Beach, *The Concept of Nature in Nineteenth-Century English Poetry* (New York: The Macmillan Co., 1936), p. 343.

63. *Works*, I, 64–65.

64. Cf. Jung, *Collected Papers on Analytical Psychology*, p. 439.

65. See Floyd Stovall, "The Value of Emerson Today," *College English*, III, No. 5 (February, 1942), 446.

66. Prescott, *The Poetic Mind*, p. 90. In this connection it is interesting to note the tendency of Emerson's thinking in what he did with the ideas of Ralph Cudworth's *The True Intellectual System of the Universe* (London: 1820 ed.). By keeping the "divine" creativeness within man himself as an extension of nature Emerson avoided Cudworth's cumbersome distinctions. In Cudworth's system "divine art" is the pure spiritual expression in the mind of God; "plastic nature" fulfills God's aims directly in the material world. But "human art" to Cudworth can be only an awkward external imitation of plastic nature. While Cudworth conceives of plastic nature as unconsciously expressing divine intentions, man is able only to consciously contrive a rough approximation of the creation in nature. On the contrary, Emerson extends the unconscious creative power into man's own creative activity, where it becomes basic as the origin of human art. See John S. Harrison, *The Teachers of Emerson* (New York: Sturgis & Walton Co., 1910), pp. 189–190; and Vivian C. Hopkins, "Emerson and Cudworth: Plastic Nature and Transcendental Art," *American Literature*, XXIII, No. 1 (March, 1951), 80–98.

67. As I see it, the unpredictable creative energy or the power of the divine spirit in man's soul — a power that Emerson called the "Will" — works through what to Emerson was "Instinct," which probably may be equated with man's "unconscious" as here used, "a certain blind wisdom, a brain of the brain, a seminal brain, which has not yet put forth organs, which rests in oversight and presence, but which seems to sheathe a certain omniscience." (*Works*, XII, 65.) Genuine artistic perceptions, then, according to Emerson, arise from the creative Will inspiring this passive Instinct to action. (*Ibid.*, 37.) The blind, passive Instinct is thus the instrument in man by which true creation may achieve its ends. This unpredictable source of creation is the glory and despair of the artist; he values most what he can least control: "And what is Inspiration? It is this Instinct, whose normal state is passive, at last put in action. We attributed power and science and good will to the Instinct, but we found it dumb and inexorable. If it would but impart itself! To coax and woo the strong Instinct to bestir itself, and work its miracle, is the end of all wise endeavor. It is resistless, and knows the way, is the inventor of all arts, and is melodious, and at all points a god. Could we prick the sides of this slumbrous giant; could we break the silence of this oldest angel, who was with God when the worlds were made! The whole art of man has been an art of excitation, to provoke, to extort speech from the drowsy genius.... All depends on some instigation, some impulse." ("Instinct and Inspiration," *Ibid.*, 68-69.) In the end, it would seem, the ordinary will of man's conscious intellect becomes most effective only when it ultimately derives its inspiration and primary direction from the deeper Will expressed through Instinct, the source of "unconscious" or "given" materials of original creation.

68. *The Poetic Mind*, p. 90.

69. See Trilling, *loc. cit.*, p. 182.

70. See Zilboorg, pp. 310–311.

71. See Jung on man's loving God in *Psychology of the Unconscious*, pp. 200–201, and Freud on the cultural inheritance of religion in *The Future of an Illusion* (London: The Hogarth Press, 1943).

## CHAPTER III

### *The Organic Language of Poetry*

1. *Memories and Studies* (New York: Longmans, Green & Co., Inc., 1911), pp. 21–22.

2. See Emerson G. Sutcliffe, "Emerson's Theories of Literary Expression," *University of Illinois Studies in Language and Literature*, VIII, No. 1 (1923).

3. P. 281.

4. Cf. Havelock Ellis, *The Dance of Life* (Boston: Houghton

Mifflin Co., 1923; New York: Random House, "Intro.," Modern Library Edition, 1929), p. 169.

5. Cf. what James Joyce says of the "epiphany" of an object in *Stephen Hero* (New York: New Directions, 1944), pp. 212–213.

6. *Works*, IX, 18.

7. Cf. Richards, *Principles of Literary Criticism*, p. 273.

8. Cf. Prescott, *The Poetic Mind*, p. 231.

9. (New York: W. W. Norton & Co., 1926), pp. 35–36.

10. *Works*, IX, 252.

11. *Ibid.*, 124.

12. *Ibid.*, III, 72.

13. *Ibid.*, II, opp. 3.

14. *Ibid.*, IX, 123.

15. *Ibid.*, 376.

16. *Ibid.*, 277.

17. *Ibid.*, 245.

18. *Ibid.*, 321–322.

19. *Ibid.*, 248. For the evolution of this poem, see *ibid.*, 484–488. The first inspiration came on the river bank, but the original rhapsody achieved its final form two years later.

## CHAPTER IV
### The Shaping Intuition

1. See Ribot, *Essay on the Creative Imagination*, p. 79.

2. See Elisabeth Schneider, *Aesthetic Motive*, p. 26.

3. See C. K. Ogden, I. A. Richards, and J. Wood, *The Foundations of Aesthetics* (New York: International Publishers, 1925), pp. 77 ff. See also Whitehead on the symbolic transfer of emotion and the suppression of irrelevant detail: "Harmonious emotion means a complex of emotions mutually intensifying; whereas the irrelevant details supply emotions which, because of their irrelevance, inhibit the main effect. Each little emotion directly arising out of some subordinate detail refuses to accept its status as a detached fact in our consciousness. It insists on its symbolic transfer to the unity of the main effect." *Symbolism, Its Meaning and Effect*, pp. 85–86.

4. Walter F. Taylor, *A History of American Letters* (New York: American Book Co., 1936), p. 154.

5. See, for example, the comment on "The Sphinx" in Ralph L. Rusk, *The Life of Ralph Waldo Emerson* (New York: Charles Scribner's Sons, 1949), p. 313. Hopkins, *Spires*, pp. 46–50, also notes some of Emerson's difficulties in poetic composition.

6. See Walter Blair, in *The Literature of the United States*, eds. Walter Blair, Theodore Hornberger, and Randall Stewart (Chicago: Scott, Foresman & Co., 1946), I, 762–765. See also Walter Blair and Clarence Faust, "Emerson's Literary Method," *Modern Philology*,

XLII, No. 2 (Nov., 1944), 79–95, in which they suggest that the organization of essays like "Art" and "The Poet," and of poems like "Each and All" and "Threnody," is based on Platonic concepts of variety and unity as Emerson interpreted them. Yet are not these concepts at least partially the result of experiencing the ways of the creative imagination as impressions, originally isolated, tend to coalesce in organic relationships molded by the psychic life? In this sense are not both Plato and Emerson poetic mythmakers?

7. Norman Foerster, in a review of Rusk's *Life of Emerson*, in *American Literature*, XXI, No. 4 (January, 1950), 496.

8. *Works*, IX, 311–314.

9. *Ibid.*, 5–6.

10. *Ibid.*, 195.

11. *Ibid.*, 38–39.

12. *Ibid.*, 28–29.

13. *Ibid.*, 33.

14. *Ibid.*, 228.

15. *Ibid.*, 42.

16. See Kathryn A. McEuen, "Emerson's Rhymes," *American Literature*, XX, No. 1 (March, 1948), 41. I agree with the whole tenor of her article.

17. Cf. some of Emerson's technical effects with those of the French Symbolists and of contemporary American poets like Ransom and MacLeish. See A. G. Lehmann, *The Symbolist Aesthetic in France, 1885–1895* (Oxford: Basil Blackwell, 1950) and Horace Gregory and Marya Zaturenska, *A History of American Poetry, 1900–1940* (New York: Harcourt, Brace & Co., 1942, 1944, 1946).

18. *Works*, III, 9–10.

19. *Ibid.*, IX, 122.

20. See *Works*, IX, 441, for the early lines from the *Journal* of 1845 which evidently were the kernel from which "Merlin" grew.

Although he does not approach the problem of the creative imagination as I do, since he sees more value in the Freudian interpretation, Daniel E. Schneider in *The Psychoanalyst and the Artist* (New York: Farrar, Straus & Co., 1950) sees the artistic work at least as the product of the unconscious, dreamlike activities of the psyche. The artistic work, in his terminology, is "dream-work 'turned inside out,' " p. 301. Cf. C. M. Bowra, *The Romantic Imagination* (Cambridge: Harvard University Press, 1949), in which he accepts connections between poetry and religion.

21. Cf. Richard Guggenheimer: "That is primarily determined by what we are and what we make of ourselves. The role of intuition is a major factor in creative thinking. Intuition is that process of thinking which attends to and recognizes the indivisible and unarrestable development that we call evolution. To intuition, the static is incon-

ceivable. Merely a symbol resorted to by the intelligence in some of its practical schemes for mastering and utilizing life forces. Intuition perceives movement and change to be the inescapable substance of being. It is the creative combination of intelligence with intuition that produces wisdom." *Creative Vision in Artist and Audience* (New York: Harper & Bros., 1950), p. 82.

22. See, for instance, *The Arts in Renewal*, ed. Sculley Bradley (Philadelphia: University of Pennsylvania Press, 1951).

23. *Works*, XI, 392.

24. Vivian Hopkins admits Emerson to the company of mystics on a broader basis than does Patrick Quinn. See Hopkins, *Spires*, Chaps. I and III, passim, and Quinn, "Emerson and Mysticism," *American Literature*, XXI, No. 4 (January, 1950), 397–414. Quinn maintains that since Emerson does not seem to have had the experience of the discipline found in an exceedingly difficult series of steps to achieve a supernatural union with God, as anyone must have according to Quinn's definition of a genuine mystic, Emerson can not accurately be called a "mystic." On the other hand, if one is content to accept as a mystic anyone who has some feeling for the working of a divine presence in his life, then Emerson qualifies. While it may be unfair to expect every "mystic" to be another St. John of the Cross, perhaps the best resolution of the problem, as far as Emerson is concerned, may be found in seeing Emerson as primarily an imaginative artist intent on presenting life's most ideal relationships. In Emerson the imagination itself becomes idealized, and thus every association and unity in an imaginative product is, in the end, "divine," for the active presence of the imagination is in itself an assurance of an avenue to man's most profound sense of his own divinity.

25. *Works*, IV, 215.

26. See Hopkins, *Spires*, p. 213.

27. *Works*, XII, 321.

28. See Hopkins, *Spires*, pp. 55–56. Rather than emphasizing an objective source of "inspiration," it seems to me, one should stress the artist's need for expression ("outlet") from the varied sources of his experiences ("inlet").

29. *Works*, X, 220.

30. *Ibid.*, 20.

31. See Hopkins, *Spires*, pp. 181–182. Emerson did not believe that the dream experience was necessarily wholly bad but rather that it allowed free play to the weaker sides of one's character. Character is the key to dreams, Emerson felt, and at times the dream may show the working of the "good genius," as Emerson called it, striving for happiness and health. Erich Fromm illustrates this better side of Emerson's interpretation of dreams in *The Forgotten Language: An Introduction to the Understanding of Dreams, Fairy Tales, and Myths*

(New York: Rinehart & Co., 1951), pp. 140–142.

32. See Hopkins, *Spires*, pp. 179–180.

33. *Works*, X, 5.

34. Hopkins shows (*Spires*, pp. 168 ff.) how this excitement some-times resulted in physical trembling, a result that we perhaps cannot regard as fully "esthetic." Although this unity of experience may not coincide entirely with the modern idea of "empathy," it at least indi-cates the more than usual degree of "sympathy" Emerson felt neces-sary between creator and observer in esthetic experience (cf. Hopkins, *Spires*, p. 173).

35. *The Complete Poetical Works of Percy Bysshe Shelley*, ed. Thomas Hutchinson (New York: Oxford University Press, 1925), p. 438.

36. See Hopkins, *Spires*, pp. 162 ff.

37. *Works*, XII, 335–336.

38. See, for example, some of the more daring experimental tenden-cies in present physics and psychology that I believe would have fascinated Emerson: Sir James Jeans, *Physics and Philosophy* (Cam-bridge: University Press, 1943), particularly his comments on "mental-ism," pp. 195 ff.; and J. B. Rhine, *The Reach of Mind* (New York: William Sloane Associates, 1947), in which he explains how through controlled experiments he has concluded there is a functional relation-ship between mind and object, pointing to what he calls an extra-physical factor in man. See esp. Chap. XII, "Consequences for Relations Among Men," pp. 204–223.

39. (New York: Harcourt, Brace & Co., 1933), pp. 176–177.

40. *Works*, III, 34.

41. Cf. Louise Bogan on a problem of modern literature, which she describes as the difficulty of humanizing outer reality, in "Mod-ernism in American Literature," *American Quarterly*, II, No. 2 (Summer, 1950), 111. See also Havelock Ellis on man's inevitable idealization of himself: "Our picture of the world, for good or for evil, is an idealised picture, a fiction, a waking dream, an *als ob*, as Vaihinger would say. But when we idealise the world we begin by first idealising ourselves. We imagine ourselves other than we are, and in so imagining, as Gaultier clearly realises, we tend to mould ourselves, so that reality becomes a prolongation of fiction." *The Dance of Life*, p. 321.

The reader who wishes to follow this point further might consult Ribot, esp. pp. 135–136; Ernst Cassirer, *Language and Myth* (New York, London: Harper & Bros., 1946); Prescott, *Poetry and Myth;* and Richard Chase, *Quest for Myth* (Baton Rouge: Louisiana State University Press, 1949). Chase particularly thinks myth depends on art. See Day-Lewis on the vitality of metaphor in his *Poetic Image*, esp. pp. 32, 106–107; he calls the poetic image the myth of the individual.

# Selected Bibliography

THESE selected readings are intended primarily to supplement works already mentioned in the notes. The first section of the bibliography includes Emerson's works, some leading criticisms of them, and biographical studies. The second section lists in separate categories selected background studies in psychology, philosophy, esthetics, and the like, which the reader may find useful in following more fully some of the points introduced in this study.

## I

ALLEN, GAY W. *American Prosody*. New York: American Book Co., 1935, pp. 91–121.

ARNOLD, MATTHEW. "Emerson," in *Discourses in America*. London: Macmillan & Co., 1885, pp. 138–207.

BEACH, JOSEPH W. "Emerson and Evolution." *University of Toronto Quarterly*, III, No. 4 (July, 1934), 474–497.

BENTON, JOEL. *Emerson as a Poet*. New York: M. F. Mansfield & A. Wessels, 1883.

BLAIR, WALTER, and FAUST, CLARENCE. "Emerson's Literary Method." *Modern Philology*, XLII, No. 2 (Nov., 1944), 79–95.

BRITTIN, NORMAN A. "Emerson and the Metaphysical Poets." *American Literature*, VIII, No. 1 (Mar., 1936), 1–21.

BROWNELL, WILLIAM C. "Emerson," in *American Prose Masters*. New York: Charles Scribner's Sons, 1909, pp. 131–204.

CABOT, JAMES E. *A Memoir of Ralph Waldo Emerson*. 2 vols. Boston: Houghton Mifflin Co., 1887.

CANBY, HENRY S. "Emerson," in *Classic Americans: A Study of Eminent American Writers from Irving to Whitman*. New York: Harcourt, Brace & Co., 1931, pp. 143–183.

CARPENTER, FREDERIC I. *Emerson and Asia*. Cambridge: Harvard University Press, 1930.

————. (ed.), *Ralph Waldo Emerson: Representative Selections, with Introduction, Bibliography, and Notes*. New York: American Book Co., 1934.

CHRISTY, ARTHUR E. *The Orient in American Transcendentalism: A Study of Emerson, Thoreau, and Alcott*. New York: Columbia University Press, 1932, pp. 61–183.

CLARK, HARRY H. "Emerson and Science." *Philological Quarterly*, X, No. 3 (July, 1931), 225–260.

EMERSON, EDWARD W. (ed.). *The Complete Works of Ralph Waldo Emerson*, Centenary Edition. 12 vols. Boston: Houghton Mifflin Co., 1903–1904.

EMERSON, EDWARD W. *Emerson in Concord*. London: Sampson Low, Marston, Searle, and Rivington, 1889.

EMERSON, EDWARD W., and FORBES, WALDO E. (eds.). *The Journals of Ralph Waldo Emerson*. 10 vols. Boston: Houghton Mifflin Co., 1909–1914.

FIRKINS, OSCAR W. *Ralph Waldo Emerson*. Boston: Houghton Mifflin Co., 1915.

FOERSTER, NORMAN. "Emerson," in *American Criticism: A Study in Literary Theory from Poe to the Present*. Boston: Houghton Mifflin Co., 1928, pp. 52–110.

————. "Emerson," in *Nature in American Literature: Studies in the Modern View of Nature*. New York: The Macmillan Co., 1923, pp. 37–68.

————. "Emerson on the Organic Principle in Art." *PMLA*, XLI, No. 1 (Mar., 1926), 193–208.

FROTHINGHAM, OCTAVIUS B. *Transcendentalism in New England*. New York: G. P. Putnam's Sons, 1876.

GAY, ROBERT M. *Emerson: A Study of the Poet as Seer*. New York: Doubleday, Doran & Co., 1928.

GODDARD, HAROLD C. *Studies in New England Transcendentalism*. New York: Columbia University Press, 1908.

GORELY, JEAN. "Emerson's Theory of Poetry." *Poetry Review*, XXII, No. 4 (July-Aug., 1931), 263–273.

GRAY, HENRY D. *Emerson: A Statement of New England Transcendentalism as Expressed in the Philosophy of Its Chief Exponent*. Palo Alto: Stanford University Press, 1917.

HARRISON, JOHN S. *The Teachers of Emerson*. New York: Sturgis & Walton Co., 1910.

HOLMES, OLIVER W. *Ralph Waldo Emerson*. Boston: Houghton Mifflin Co., 1884.

HUBBELL, GEORGE S. *A Concordance to the Poems of Ralph Waldo Emerson*. New York: The H. W. Wilson Co., 1932.

JORGENSON, CHESTER E. "Emerson's Paradise under the Shadow of Swords." *Philological Quarterly*, XI, No. 3 (July, 1932), 274–292.

KREYMBORG, ALFRED. "The Intoxicated Emerson," in *Our Singing Strength: An Outline of American Poetry (1620–1930)*. New York: Coward-McCann, Inc., 1929, pp. 67–83.

MARCHAND, ERNEST. "Emerson and the Frontier." *American Literature*, III, No. 2 (May, 1931), 149–174.

MATTHIESSEN, F. O. *American Renaissance: Art and Expression in the Age of Emerson and Whitman*. New York: Oxford University Press, 1941, pp. 3–75.

MICHAUD, RÉGIS. *L'Esthétique d'Emerson: La Nature, L'Art, L'Histoire*. Paris: Librairie Félix Alcan, 1931.

MORE, PAUL E. "Emerson," in *Cambridge History of American Literature*. New York: G. P. Putnam's Sons, 1917, I, 349–362.

NOYES, ALFRED. "The Poetry of Emerson," in *Some Aspects of Mod-

*ern Poetry*. New York: Frederick A. Stokes Co., 1924, pp. 65–78.

PARRINGTON, VERNON L. "Emerson, Transcendental Critic," in *The Romantic Revolution in America*. New York: Harcourt, Brace & Co., 1927, pp. 386–399.

PERRY, BLISS. *Emerson Today*. Princeton: Princeton University Press, 1931.

PETTIGREW, RICHARD C. "Emerson and Milton." *American Literature*, III, No. 1 (Mar., 1931), 45–59.

RUSK, RALPH L. (ed.). *The Letters of Ralph Waldo Emerson*. 6 vols. New York: Columbia University Press, 1939.

——. *The Life of Ralph Waldo Emerson*. New York: Charles Scribner's Sons, 1949.

SANTAYANA, GEORGE. "Emerson," in *Interpretations of Poetry and Religion*. New York: Charles Scribner's Sons, 1900, pp. 217–233.

SHERMAN, STUART P. "The Emersonian Liberation," in *Americans*. New York: Charles Scribner's Sons, 1922, pp. 63–121.

STEDMAN, EDMUND C. "Emerson," in *Poets of America*. Boston: Houghton Mifflin Co., 1885, pp. 133–179.

STOVALL, FLOYD. "The Value of Emerson Today." *College English*, III, No. 5 (Feb., 1942), 442–454.

SUTCLIFFE, EMERSON G. "Emerson's Theories of Literary Expression," *University of Illinois Studies in Language and Literature*, VIII, No. 1, 1923.

THOMPSON, FRANK T. "Emerson and Carlyle." *Studies in Philology*, XXIV, No. 3 (July, 1927), 438–453.

——. "Emerson's Indebtedness to Coleridge." *Studies in Philology*, XXIII, No. 1 (Jan., 1926), 55–76.

——. "Emerson's Theory and Practice of Poetry." *PMLA*, XLIII, No. 4 (Dec., 1928), 1170–1184.

WAHR, FREDERICK B. *Emerson and Goethe*. Ann Arbor: G. Wahr, 1915.

WOODBERRY, GEORGE E. *Ralph Waldo Emerson*. New York: The Macmillan Co., 1907.

YOUNG, CHARLES L. *Emerson's Montaigne*. New York: The Macmillan Co., 1941.

ZINK, HARRIET R. "Emerson's Use of the Bible." *University of Nebraska Studies in Language, Literature and Criticism*, XIV, 1935.

# II

## A. PSYCHOLOGY

BAUDOUIN, CHARLES. *Psychoanalysis and Aesthetics*. New York: Dodd, Mead & Co., 1924.

DOWNEY, JUNE E. *Creative Imagination: Studies in the Psychology of Literature*. New York: Harcourt, Brace & Co., 1929.

EMERSON, L. E. "Emerson and Freud." *Psychoanalytic Review*, XX, No. 2 (April, 1933), 208–214.

FREUD, SIGMUND. *The Ego and the Id*. International Psychoanalytical Library, ed. Ernest Jones, XII. London: The Hogarth Press, 1927.

———. *The Future of an Illusion*. London: The Hogarth Press, 1943

GHISELIN, BREWSTER. (ed.). *The Creative Process: A Symposium*. Berkeley and Los Angeles: University of California Press, 1952.

JAMES, WILLIAM. *The Principles of Psychology*. 2 vols. New York: Henry Holt & Co., 1890.

JUNG, CARL G. *Collected Papers on Analytical Psychology*. New York: Moffat, Yard & Co. [now Dodd, Mead & Co.], 1917.

———. *The Integration of Personality*. New York: Farrar and Rinehart, 1939.

———. *Modern Man in Search of a Soul*. New York: Harcourt, Brace & Co., 1933.

———. *Psychology and Religion*. New Haven: Yale University Press, 1938.

———. *Psychology of the Unconscious: A Study of the Trans-formations and Symbolisms of the Libido, A Contribution to the History of the Evolution of Thought*. New York: Moffat, Yard & Co. [now Dodd, Mead & Co.], 1916.

LEWIS, CLIVE S. "Psycho-analysis and Literary Criticism," in *Essays and Studies by Members of The English Association*. Oxford: Clarendon Press, 1942, XXVII, 7–21.

RHINE, J. B. *The Reach of Mind*. New York: William Sloane Associ-ates, 1947.

RIBOT, THÉODULE. *Essay on the Creative Imagination*. Chicago: The Open Court Publishing Co.; London: Kegan Paul, Trench, Trubner & Co., 1906.

SACHS, HANNS. *The Creative Unconscious: Studies in the Psycho-analysis of Art*. Cambridge, Mass.: Sci-Art Publishers, 1942.

SPEARMAN, CHARLES E. *Creative Mind*. New York: D. Appleton & Co.; Cambridge: University Press, 1931.

WASHBURN, MARGARET F. *Movement and Mental Imagery*. Boston: Houghton Mifflin Co., 1916.

ZILBOORG, GREGORY. *Mind, Medicine, and Man*. New York: Harcourt, Brace & Co., 1943.


B. PHILOSOPHY

BERGSON, HENRI. *Creative Evolution*. New York: Henry Holt & Co., 1911; Random House, 1944.

———. *The Creative Mind*. New York: Philosophical Library, 1946.

DU NOÜY, LECOMTE. *Human Destiny*. New York: Longmans, Green & Co., 1947.

ELLIS, HAVELOCK. *The Dance of Life*. Boston: Houghton Mifflin Co., 1923; New York: Random House, "Intro.," 1929.

HOSPERS, JOHN. *Meaning and Truth in the Arts*. Chapel Hill: University of North Carolina Press, 1946.

HUXLEY, ALDOUS. *The Perennial Philosophy*. New York: Harper & Bros., 1944, 1945.

INGE, WILLIAM R. *The Philosophy of Plotinus*. 2 vols. London, New York: Longmans, Green & Co., 1918.

————. *The Religious Philosophy of Plotinus and Some Modern Philosophies of Religion*. London: Lindsey Press, [1914?].

JEANS, JAMES. *Physics and Philosophy*. Cambridge: University Press; New York: The Macmillan Co., 1943.

LANGER, SUSANNE K. *Philosophy in a New Key: A Study in the Symbolism of Reason, Rite, and Art*. Cambridge: Harvard University Press, 1942.

NORTHROP, F. S. C. *The Logic of the Sciences and the Humanities*. New York: The Macmillan Co., 1947.

SCHNEIDER, HERBERT W. *A History of American Philosophy*. New York: Columbia University Press, 1946. ("Emerson," pp. 280–286.)

WHITEHEAD, ALFRED N. *Symbolism, Its Meaning and Effect*. New York: The Macmillan Co., 1927.

WHYTE, LANCELOT L. *The Next Development in Man*. New York: Henry Holt & Co., 1948.

### C. ESTHETIC THEORY

ABERCROMBIE, LASCELLES. *The Theory of Poetry*. New York: Harcourt, Brace & Co., 1926.

ALEXANDER, SAMUEL. *Beauty and Other Forms of Value*. London: Macmillan & Co., 1933.

ARNHEIM, RUDOLPH, AUDEN, W. H., SHAPIRO, KARL, and STAUFFER, DONALD A. *Poets at Work: Essays Based on the Modern Poetry Collection at the Lockwood Memorial Library, University of Buffalo*. New York: Harcourt, Brace & Co., 1948.

BROOKS, CLEANTH. *Modern Poetry and the Tradition*. Chapel Hill: University of North Carolina Press, 1939.

CROCE, BENEDETTO. *Aesthetic as Science of Expression and General Linguistic*. London: Macmillan & Co., 1922.

DEWEY, JOHN. *Art as Experience*. New York: Minton, Balch & Co., 1934.

FAURE, ELIE. *The Spirit of the Forms*. New York: Harper & Bros., 1930; Garden City: Garden City Publishing Co., 1937.

GILBERT, KATHERINE. *Studies in Recent Aesthetic*. Chapel Hill: University of North Carolina Press, 1927.

GUGGENHEIMER, RICHARD. *Creative Vision in Artist and Audience*. New York: Harper & Bros., 1950.

HOPKINS, VIVIAN C. *Spires of Form: A Study of Emerson's Aes-*

*thetic Theory*. Cambridge: Harvard University Press, 1951.

HULME, THOMAS E. *Speculations: Essays on Humanism and the Philosophy of Art*. London: Kegan Paul, Trench, Trubner & Co.; New York: Harcourt, Brace & Co., 1936.

LUNDHOLM, HELGE. *The Aesthetic Sentiment: A Criticism and an Original Excursion*. Cambridge, Mass.: Sci-Art Publishers, 1941.

OGDEN, C. K., RICHARDS, I. A., and WOOD, J. *The Foundations of Aesthetics*. New York: International Publishers, 1925.

PARKER, DeWITT H. *The Principles of Aesthetics*. Boston, New York: Silver, Burdett & Co., 1920.

POTTLE, FREDERICK A. *The Idiom of Poetry*. Ithaca: Cornell University Press, 1946.

PRESCOTT, FREDERICK C. *The Poetic Mind*. New York: The Macmillan Co., 1922.

RICHARDS, I. A. *Coleridge on Imagination*. London: Kegan Paul, Trench, Trubner & Co., 1934.

SCHNEIDER, ELISABETH. *Aesthetic Motive*. New York: The Macmillan Co., 1939.

STAUFFER, DONALD A. *The Nature of Poetry*. New York: W. W. Norton & Co., 1946.

TATE, ALLEN. (ed.). *The Language of Poetry*. Princeton: University Press; London: H. Milford, Oxford University Press, 1942.

### D. MYSTICISM

BENNETT, CHARLES A. *A Philosophical Study of Mysticism: An Essay*. New Haven: Yale University Press, 1923.

HUGHES, THOMAS H. *The Philosophic Basis of Mysticism*. Edinburgh: T. & T. Clark, 1937.

MUKERJEE, RADHAKAMAL. *Theory and Art of Mysticism*. London, New York: Longmans, Green & Co., 1937.

RUSSELL, BERTRAND. *Mysticism and Logic and Other Essays*. London: Longmans, Green & Co., 1918.

SILBERER, HERBERT. *Problems of Mysticism and Its Symbolism*. New York: Moffat, Yard & Co., 1917.

UNDERHILL, EVELYN. *The Mystic Way: A Psychological Study in Christian Origins*. London: J. M. Dent & Sons; New York: E. P. Dutton & Co., 1913.

### E. MYTHOLOGY

CALVERTON, VICTOR F. (ed.). *The Making of Man: An Outline of Anthropology*. New York: Random House, 1931.

CASSIRER, ERNST. *Language and Myth*. New York, London: Harper & Bros., 1946.

FRAZER, JAMES G. *The Golden Bough: A Study in Magic and Religion*. 12 vols. (3rd ed.). London: Macmillan & Co., 1907–1920.

HAWKRIDGE, EMMA. *The Wisdom Tree*. Boston: Houghton Mifflin Co., 1945.

PRESCOTT, FREDERICK C. *Poetry and Myth*. New York: The Macmillan Co., 1927.

F. LITERARY CRITICISM (General)

BARTLETT, PHYLLIS. *Poems in Process*. New York: Oxford University Press, 1951.

BARZUN, JACQUES. *Romanticism and the Modern Ego*. Boston: Little, Brown & Co., 1943.

BEACH, JOSEPH W. *The Concept of Nature in Nineteenth-Century English Poetry*. New York: The Macmillan Co., 1936.

COLERIDGE, SAMUEL T. *Biographia Literaria or Biographical Sketches of My Literary Life and Opinions*, ed. John Calvin Metcalf. New York: The Macmillan Co., 1926.

DAY-LEWIS, CECIL. *The Poetic Image*. New York: Oxford University Press, 1947.

EMPSON, WILLIAM. *Seven Types of Ambiguity: A Study of Its Effects in English Verse*. London: Chatto and Windus, 1930.

FIRKINS, OSCAR W. *Power and Elusiveness in Shelley*. Minneapolis: University of Minnesota Press, 1937.

FOGLE, RICHARD H. *The Imagery of Keats and Shelley: A Comparative Study*. Chapel Hill: University of North Carolina Press, 1949.

GREENE, THEODORE M. *The Arts and the Art of Criticism*. Princeton: Princeton University Press, 1947.

O'CONNER, WILLIAM V. "Symbolism and the Study of Poetry." *College English*, VII, No. 7 (April, 1946), 374–379.

PEPPER, STEPHEN C. *The Basis of Criticism in the Arts*. Cambridge: Harvard University Press, 1945.

RICHARDS, I. A. *Principles of Literary Criticism*. New York: Harcourt, Brace & Co., 1925.

————. *Science and Poetry*. New York: W. W. Norton & Co., 1926.

RUGOFF, MILTON A. *Donne's Imagery: A Study in Creative Sources*. New York: Corporate Press, 1939.

SPURGEON, CAROLINE. *Shakespeare's Imagery and What It Tells Us*. Cambridge: University Press; New York: The Macmillan Co., 1935.

TUVE, ROSEMOND. *Elizabethan and Metaphysical Imagery: Renaissance Poetic and Twentieth-Century Critics*. Chicago: University of Chicago Press, 1947.

WELLS, HENRY W. *The American Way of Poetry*. New York: Columbia University Press, 1943.

WINTERS, YVOR. *Maule's Curse: Seven Studies in the History of American Obscurantism*. Norfolk, Conn.: New Directions, 1938. ("Jones Very and R. W. Emerson: Aspects of New England Mysticism," pp. 125–146.)

# Index

112-18
156

# DATE DUE

| | | | |
|---|---|---|---|
| | | | |
| | | | |
| | | | |
| | | | |
| | | | |
| | | | |
| | | | |
| | | | |
| | | | |
| | | | |
| | | | |
| | | | |
| | | | |
| | | | |
| | | | |
| | | | |
| | | | |
| | | | |
| | | | |
| GAYLORD | | | PRINTED IN U.S.A. |